100 THINGS
EAGLES FANS
SHOULD KNOW & DO
BEFORE THEY DIE

100 THINGS EAGLES FANS
SHOULD KNOW & DO
BEFORE THEY DIE

Chuck Carlson

TRIUMPH
BOOKS

The Library of Congress has catalogued the previous edition as follows:

Carlson, Chuck, 1957–
  100 things Eagles fans should know & do before they die / Chuck Carlson.
    p. cm.
  Includes bibliographical references.

1. Philadelphia Eagles (Football team)—History. 2. Philadelphia Eagles (Football team)—Miscellanea. I. Title. II. Title: One hundred things Eagles fans should know & do before they die.
  GV956.P44C37 2011
  796.332'640974811—dc23

                              2011029106

This book is available in quantity at special discounts for your group or organization. For further information, contact:
  Triumph Books LLC
  814 North Franklin Street
  Chicago, Illinois 60610
  (312) 337-0747
  www.triumphbooks.com

Printed in U.S.A.
ISBN: 978-1-62937-617-2
Design by Patricia Frey
Photos courtesy of AP Images

*This book is dedicated to the fans of the
Philadelphia Eagles. Your time has finally come.*

*Thanks to my son Patrick
for valuable editorial assistance.*

Contents

Introduction

As an epic and unforgettable Super Bowl LII came to a close in Minneapolis, Minnesota, in February 2018, the only question facing this star-crossed franchise and its tortured fan base was how their hearts would be torn out this time.

It was going to happen, because it always did. Wasn't that the age-old philosophy of angst for the Philadelphia Eagles, a team that always seemed to be on the outside looking in?

So on the final play of a game that saw more than 1,100 yards of offense pile up between the Eagles and the New England Patriots, and which had seen the scrappy Eagles retake a 41–33 lead, those who knew history knew this impending heartache might be the worst of all.

That's when Tom Brady, New England's peerless quarterback who had thrown for an ungodly 505 yards in the game, reared back for one last desperation pass and the perfect, tragic ending seemed ready to play out.

The ball cut through the air of U.S. Bank Stadium toward the end zone where three Patriots receivers and six Eagles defenders waited. One of those Patriots, maybe Rob Gronkowski, would muscle up to make the catch, or maybe Chris Hogan would catch a deflection off the hands of a hapless Eagles defender.

It would be a miraculous TD that would suck the air out of the stadium, out of the Eagles, and out of their long-suffering fans. The resulting two-point conversion would be expected and would tie the game, sending it into an overtime that New England would dominate. Another Super Bowl for the Patriots. And the Eagles? Well, they played hard.

And that would be that. Heartbreak City for Philly.

Again.

Minneapolis, Minnesota, February 4, 2018: Doug Pederson holds up the Lombardi Trophy after the Eagles defeated the Patriots 41–33 in Super Bowl LII. (Perry Knotts via AP)

But something strange and wondrous and unexpected happened. As most of Philadelphia covered its eyes waiting for the result of that pass, nothing from their darkest dreams transpired.

After staying in the air seemingly forever, the ball pinballed off three players and, finally, hit the ground. Incomplete.

That was it. For a second there was nothing, just amazed silence. And then there wasn't.

Silence was replaced by eruptions of pure joy. The Philadelphia Eagles were champions of the NFL for the first time since 1960, and for the longest time no one really knew how to react. From Philadelphia to New Jersey to Delaware and across Pennsylvania (maybe even Pittsburgh?) and the country, Eagles fans had thought they knew how they'd react if and when their Eagles finally won it all. But this was something new, something foreign, something completely unexpected.

Pure joy.

For years, for decades, for lifetimes really, those who followed and played for the Eagles have always wondered what a championship would feel like, and now it was here.

"We're champions for life," said defensive end Brandon Graham, who made perhaps the play of the game for the Eagles when he forced a Brady fumble with less than two minutes to play, when it seemed the Patriots were ready to reassert themselves.

Such was the Philadelphia Eagles' road to the championship. Fraught with detours that would have stopped other teams, these Eagles found a way when few others thought they could. And that's what these Eagles will be remembered for.

This is one of those stories with a happy ending, even for football fans who don't know much about the Eagles and their rugged history. This is a franchise born at the dawn of the NFL, when giants like George Halas and Curly Lambeau roamed the sidelines.

It has been one of the premier franchises in the NFL for years, producing larger-than-life players like Norm Van Brocklin and

Steve Van Buren and Reggie White and to a lesser extent, Sonny Jurgensen and Mike Ditka.

It has produced good, but not great, teams over the years and it has operated just outside the circle of those franchises that have become part of NFL lore.

All that was missing, it seemed, was a Super Bowl title. Two other trips to the championship ended in disappointment and, in truth, these Eagles were underdogs to the powerful Patriots.

But with an underrated and innovative head coach, a backup quarterback with a unquenchable belief in himself, and a cast of role players with a lot to prove, they became a team in far more than name alone.

Now the Eagles have their Super Bowl title and a new place, a new view of the NFL pantheon. They now sit alongside a precious few who have accomplished something special and, as they are already figuring out, the view is truly magnificent.

—Chuck Carlson
February 2018

1 Eagles Fans

All of a sudden it's gotten a little easier to be a Philadelphia Eagles fan. It's amazing what a Super Bowl victory can do. Still, there will always be something that makes following this team a challenge.

Ask any of them. It has never been a picnic, even when it should have been; even when they knew they had the best team in football; even when they knew all the stars were aligning properly for their team to finally do something special.

Even with all that they knew something bad would happen. Whether it was Super Bowl XV in January 1981, when the Eagles looked shell-shocked and dazed against the Oakland Raiders; or Super Bowl XXXIX in February 2005 against the New England Patriots; or even in the final minutes of that glorious Super Bowl LII. It goes with the territory. To be an Eagles fan is to always hope for the best, expect the worst, and know something will always be better a little further down the road.

The team has one of the NFL's top pedigrees, equal in stature historically to some of the game's storied franchises in Green Bay, Chicago, and New York. Throughout history the team has featured some of the game's best players—from Steve Van Buren, Norm Van Brocklin, and Sonny Jurgensen to Wilbert Montgomery, Ron Jaworski, and Harold Carmichael all the way to star-crossed Reggie White and Jerome Brown—and continues that tradition of excellence today with the likes of Michael Vick and DeShaun Jackson.

There is an unusual relationship between players and fans—antagonistic, loving, and confrontational all at the same time. And for generations, Eagles players have marveled at the way fans can make booing almost an art form.

1

Booing Santa Claus? Snow Kidding.

Lost in the mist of time, myth, history, and rumor is the story—repeated ad nauseam and with great enthusiasm—that Philadelphia sports fans are so tough and so unrelenting that they even booed Santa Claus. But did it really happen, or is it just a great tale to drive home the point about Philly fans?

On December 15, 1968, at the old Franklin Field, a bad Eagles team faced the Minnesota Vikings on a cold, snowy, windy, lousy day that matched the mood of many Eagles fans. It had been a horrendous season that began badly and had only gotten worse.

Philly started the season with 11 straight losses. Then, almost to make matters worse, the Eagles won their next two games to take themselves out of the running for the NFL's No. 1 draft pick—which, that year, proved to be a pretty good running back from the University of Southern California named O.J. Simpson.

At halftime of the Vikings game, Eagles officials had plans to put on a Christmas extravaganza that would melt the hearts of even the most cynical fans. Santa Claus would ride onto the field in a sleigh pulled by eight fiberglass reindeer while the Eagles cheerleaders dressed up as elves. What wasn't there to like?

Well, the float got stuck in the mud and never made it on the field, and the Santa Claus hired for the gig was nowhere to be found. In desperation, an Eagles PR guy pulled a fan who was already dressed as Santa for the occasion out of the stands as a stand-in.

Frank Olivo, who died in 2015 at age 66, was dressed in red corduroy and a fake beard; the Eagles staff supplied him with a sack, and he walked around the stadium waving to the fans as the band played "Here Comes Santa Claus."

The 54,000 or so fans on hand were not impressed, so the boos rained down on the poor guy. And did we mention the snowballs?

"Oh yeah, I was pelted," Olivo said later.

Boos and snowballs. For Santa. Merry Christmas.

No one ever did find the Santa who was supposed to appear. Olivo took it all with good humor and will go down in history as the subject of one of the greatest stories in NFL history.

Oh, and the Eagles lost the game 24–17, marking the second of 11 straight seasons in which the team was .500 or worse.

"Philly is a tough town," said quarterback Sonny Jurgensen, who played seven seasons for the Eagles and can sometimes still hear the boos. "You're out there trying to win, trying to do good, and they boo. Why?"

It's a good question without a simple answer. Eagles fans are passionate and critical and demanding and frustrated. After all, their Eagles still have no Super Bowl title and have only appeared twice. The team has won three NFL championships but none since 1960. They have been close since then but not close enough. The fans have seen teams destined for greatness fall apart at the worst time and superb players fail in the clutch. And yes, they have watched a lot of bad football over the years too, much of it played in archaic bandboxes like Franklin Field and Veterans Stadium.

Many opposing players truly hated going to Philly to play the Eagles. Though it cannot be denied: playing before Eagles fans was an experience to remember.

"It's a place I grew to really like in a distorted, perverted way," said longtime New York Giants coach Bill Parcells. "It's a place where they let you know what they thought of you, and it was almost always in very negative terms. But the more they [abused] you, the more you began to understand that it was part of a respect they had for you."

The stories are legendary. There was the booing of Santa Claus and the fusillade of snowballs that rained down on the Dallas Cowboys in 1989. There were warnings that parents shouldn't bring their kids to the Vet for games because the place was too dangerous and too rowdy. There were arrests and confrontations with players in the parking lot after games. There was the game during which Cowboys receiver Michael Irvin was taken off the field with a spinal cord injury that ultimately ended his career in 1999—and Eagles fans cheered.

It has changed a lot since the Eagles moved into the more palatial Lincoln Financial Field in 2003. Much of the riffraff has been identified and removed. Going to an Eagles game today is still an experience, but it's no longer a trip through the minefield it once was.

The Eagles continued to come close to the pinnacle, reaching a hand to the summit, only to be denied at the end. The latest incarnation of that risk-reward-regret came in 2010 when the Eagles used the MVP-type season of one of the NFL's great reclamation projects, quarterback Michael Vick, to win an NFC East title with a 10–6 record.

That title was all but sewn up in a remarkable game December 19 on the road against the hated New York Giants. Trailing most of the game, the Eagles rallied to score 28 points in the fourth quarter behind Vick. Then, on the game's final play, DeSean Jackson gathered in a punt, navigated through three great blocks, and brought the kick back 65 yards for the winning touchdown. His celebratory half-gainer into the end zone will never be forgotten by Eagles fans—or by Giants fans, for that matter.

The Eagles went on to win the division title, but in the first round of playoffs they fell victim to the rolling thunder that proved to be the Green Bay Packers and their relentless Super Bowl run. Even so, the Eagles had their opportunities. But two missed field goals and a Vick interception in the end zone during the final minute ended yet another frustrating season.

For Eagles fans, there was always supposed to be next season. And even with that long-sought Super Bowl championship in 2017, in many ways there always will be.

Those Championship Eagles

The 2017 Philadelphia Eagles, in many ways, defied explanation.

It was a team from which not much was expected, led by a quarterback from whom little had been seen and a head coach who many thought was in over his head. It was a team that had little margin for error even in the best of circumstances and, in most ways, those circumstances were not ideal. And it was a team that, in an NFL season roiled by social and racial issues, stood tall and together and defiant.

"We are trying to do things the right way both on and off the field," wide receiver Torrey Smith told CNN during the season.

Without doubt, it was the adversity that made these Eagles stronger, and when it turned out they were underdogs in every playoff game, despite being the NFC's top seed, it was just more fuel for that righteous indignation.

If some teams perform with chips on their shoulders, the Eagles played with boulders on theirs.

Indeed, when the Eagles had conquered the New England Patriots in Super Bowl LII, coach Doug Pederson stood in front of his players and roared, "This is a team game and we said before, an individual can make a difference…"

And all at once his players responded, "But a team makes a miracle!"

Perhaps the Eagles "miracle" was born from the chaos and disappointment of the previous season.

Featuring a new quarterback, Carson Wentz, the second pick in the 2016 NFL Draft, and a rookie coach in Pederson, those Eagles started 3–0 before losing nine of 11 games to fall out of playoff contention. But most important, Pederson kept his team together and they won their final two games to finish 7–9.

It wasn't great, but it was a sign of a team that didn't give up. And in the offseason, general manager Howie Roseman began constructing the pieces for the 2017 season.

It began March 9, when the Eagles signed two free agent wide receivers, the disillusioned and disappointing former Chicago Bear Alshon Jeffery and Smith, who had played well for the Baltimore Ravens and then spent the previous two season with the 49ers. They provided Wentz with two targets he did not have as a rookie.

On March 13, the Eagles brought back quarterback Nick Foles to back up Wentz. The move barely registered, especially since Foles, after his remarkable 2013 when he threw 27 touchdown passes and just two interceptions and led the Eagles to the playoffs, had faded into obscurity. He'd been traded in 2015 to the Rams and then went to the Chiefs, where he considered retiring. So his return to Philly seemed more like filling a spot than counting on him to contribute.

The Eagles kept making moves, signing two more free agents in cornerback Patrick Robinson and defensive end Chris Long at the end of March and trading a third round draft pick to the Baltimore Ravens for defensive tackle Timmy Jernigan.

In May, the Eagles signed free agent running back LaGarrette Blount. In August, they traded with Buffalo for cornerback Ronald Darby. Then, in October, with Miami for running back Jay Ajayi,

Those moves proved to be strokes of genius, as all contributed mightily to Philly's success, especially in the postseason.

Those moves, coupled with the players already on the team, provided just the right chemistry. But they had something else— something that was harder to quantify and nearly impossible to label. And they would need all of it in a season like few others.

The Eagles were not immune to setbacks, as all-everything running back Darren Sproles, in the third game of the season, broke his arm and tore his anterior cruciate ligament on the same play, ending his season. Shortly after, linebacker Jason Hicks, their best defensives player, suffered a torn Achilles tendon and was also lost for the season.

But the Eagles weathered those storms and roared to a 10–2 record behind quarterback Carson Wentz, who was building an impressive case for NFL Most Valuable Player.

All that seemed to change in a key battle with the Los Angeles Rams when Wentz, diving into the end zone for a touchdown (that would be nullified by an Eagles penalty) suffered a torn ACL and posterior cruciate ligament in his left knee.

And in the blink of an eye—or in the time it takes for a knee ligament to tear—the Philadelphia Eagles went from the dominant team in the NFC and Super Bowl favorites to hard-luck pretenders.

Pederson looked dazed on the postgame podium as he discussed the injury. He looked even worse the next day when the diagnosis was confirmed. Their MVP candidate was done for the season.

The Eagles players and coaches said all the right things about pulling together and having the next man step up and do his job, but whether they believed it or not remained to be seen.

Nick Foles, the afterthought signing in March, was now going to lead the Eagles again.

"I had confidence in myself and so did all my teammates," he said.

"I am very confident in that, just by the way the guys have handled their business the last two weeks, the way we practiced last week and the way we prepared this week," Pederson said. "Does that guarantee anything? No. We've still got to go out and play, but just the attitude of the team…focused on the opponent this week."

But for Eagles fans who had always been waiting for the other shoe to drop? This was all but expected. Another great season ruined by cruel fate. Time to look at next season…

But a funny thing happened to the Eagles on their way to oblivion. They went on to post a 13–3 regular season record and gain the top seed in the NFC playoffs. But they were limping and damaged and were underdogs in the postseason, a status that infuriated the Eagles.

"We're not underdogs to anybody," Long said. "It's an insult."

But perhaps it's off the field where the Eagles endeared themselves to many people. Led by Smith, Long, and safety Malcolm Jenkins, the Eagles showed there was more to being NFL players than what they accomplished on the field.

Indeed, when Jenkins was asked by CNN in November about his social causes, he laughed.

"How much time you got?" he said.

He spoke about his ridealongs with the Philadelphia Police Department that involved shootings, his various keynote speeches and panel discussions on racial issues, his meetings with NFL commissioner Roger Goodell as a leader of the newly established Players Coalition, his meetings with prison reform groups, and more.

Long donated his game checks to his hometown of Charlottesville, Virginia, to help the healing from the racially charged protests earlier in the year and also formed Long's Waterboys, which provides clean water to villages in East Africa as well as working with American military veterans.

Smith, among other activities, created a scholarship for low-income schools.

To Long, it's the least that can be done.

"It proves that you can pursue some of the things you care about off the field and still win," he said.

And they did win. Behind the rejuvenated Foles, a dominating defense, and the play of both returning veterans and those players picked up along the way, the Eagles knocked off the Atlanta Falcons in the first round of the playoffs, crushed the Minnesota

Vikings in the NFC Championship Game, and, of course, played fearlessly in upsetting the Patriots in the Super Bowl.

In those three playoffs games, Foles was magnificent, throwing for 971 yards and six touchdowns. Ajayi ran for 184 yards on 42 carries and caught six passes. Jeffery caught 12 passes for 219 yards and three touchdowns. Smith caught 13 passes for 157 yards and a score, and Blount torched his former team, the Patriots, for 90 rushing yards and a touchdown.

"We all believed," Jenkins said. "I love these guys."

Called the most "woke" team in the NFL, these Eagles showed that a team can believe in themselves and in their mission but can also believe in the things in the world that truly matter.

And maybe that's what a team is really supposed to be.

Birth of the Eagles

What would become the National Football League really got its start in 1920 with the formation of the American Professional Football Association, a loose confederation of 14 teams, most of them based in Ohio.

In 1922 the APFA was renamed the National Football League and, by 1924, there were 18 franchises in such far-flung places as Green Bay, Wisconsin; Hammond, Indiana; Duluth, Minnesota; Chicago, Illinois; and the Frankford section of Philadelphia. Named the Yellow Jackets, the Philly team "won" the league title with an 11–2–1 record that year.

In 1925 five new franchises entered the league—the New York Giants, Detroit Panthers, Canton Bulldogs, Providence Steam Roller, and Pottsville Maroons.

Late that season, Frankford, with Philadelphia as its home territory, and Pottsville, which covered the Pittsburgh area, were embroiled in a controversy that still lingers to this day.

Pottsville and the Chicago Cardinals were the best teams in the league that year, and the Maroons appeared to prove it with a decisive late-season win over the Cardinals. But in those days, NFL teams were a lot like barnstormers, going wherever they could and playing whomever challenged them for the money every fledgling franchise desperately needed.

In December the Maroons scheduled a game against a collection of former Notre Dame stars, including the legendary Four Horsemen. The problem was that the game was scheduled at Philadelphia's Shibe Park, violating Frankford's territorial rights. The Maroons were also scheduled to play the Yellow Jackets that same day and, as a result, Frankford lodged a protest.

The Maroons were warned by league officials not to play the Notre Dame exhibition but did anyway. The result? Pottsville was stripped of its league title and the franchise was suspended the following year. The Cardinals were offered the title but refused it, claiming the Maroons had beaten them fairly and squarely earlier that month.

The Cards are still listed as the 1925 league champions, but in 2003 the issue was reopened in an effort to return the title to the Maroons. NFL owners voted 30–2 not to revisit the issue, and the only dissenting votes belonged to Eagles owner Jeffrey Lurie and Steelers head man Dan Rooney.

Frankford remained a member of the NFL until 1931, when it finally folded. In 1933 a syndicate headed by Bert Bell and Lud Wray paid a $25,000 franchise fee and placed a team in Philadelphia. They named the new team the Eagles in honor of the symbol of the New Deal's National Recovery Act instituted by President Franklin D. Roosevelt in an effort to get America out of the Depression.

And thus began the story of a franchise that continues to make its own brand of history.

4 Carson Wentz and Nick Foles

They represent, in more ways than one, the past, present, and future of the Philadelphia Eagles.

They are Nick Foles and Carson Wentz, the once and future stars of the Eagles, each of whom did their part in bringing a Super Bowl championship to the city in 2017.

Without each other, none of what transpired that season might have happened. After all it was Wentz, the heralded second pick from the 2016 NFL Draft playing so superbly through the first three and half months of the season, who put the Eagles in the right position and gave them the badly needed belief that they could be great. And it was Foles, back after three years of NFL anonymity, who rode a wave of self-confidence to bring the Eagles all the way to the championship.

Wentz, clearly, is the future of the Philadelphia Eagles. In his second season as the starter, he was piling up the kind of numbers that made him a legitimate league MVP candidate.

He was becoming the face, heart, and the soul of the franchise and for the first time in years, long-suffering fans saw the player who could take their Eagles where they needed to go. Through fewer than 13 games, Wentz had thrown for 3,296 yards with 33 touchdowns and only seven interceptions and the Eagles had the best record in the NFC.

Wentz had it all. At 6'5" and 240 pounds, he had the size and strength and controlled arrogance that every Super Bowl contender needed. Indeed, even after he suffered his season-ending left knee injury in 2017, his final play was a touchdown pass. And in less than two seasons as the starter, Wentz already had five team passing records—and more figured to come.

But his injury devastated the Eagles and their fan base. Even head coach Doug Pederson, when announcing the extent of the injury two days later, was shaken. Injuries in the NFL are part of the gig, but some injuries are worse than others and many observers figured this was the end of yet another dream.

That was the void Foles stepped into. Signed the previous off-season to provide some semblance of experience behind Wentz, Foles had to convince himself he still wanted to play.

He'd had a great rookie season under coach Chip Kelly in Philadelphia in 2013. But it had gone downhill quickly since. He was traded in 2015 to St. Louis, then, discouraged by the situation there, sought his release and signed with Kansas City.

But along the way, Foles wrestled with self doubt and an uncertainty if he even wanted to play anymore.

After a year in Kansas City, he signed again with the Eagles, convinced he still had what it took to make a contribution in the league.

With Wentz's support, Foles took over the Eagles' quest, and while it wasn't always smooth, he found his way and the Eagles followed along.

It culminated with his Super Bowl performance, in which he completed 28 of 43 passes for 373 yards and three touchdowns, earning him MVP honors.

Months after he'd wondered if he had a future in the league, he had reached goals even he hadn't imagined. And what endeared him to fan everywhere was his appreciation for it all.

"I think as people, we deal with struggles," he said. "I'm grateful that I made the decision to come back and play."

With his performance, Foles set himself up to become a starter anywhere in the league. Wentz remains the present and the future of an Eagles team heading in a direction it's never known before.

And for both quarterbacks, it's a good place to be.

5 Bert Bell

There would be no National Football League without the foresight, guts, hubris, and chutzpah of a few remarkable individuals. History has chronicled many of them in glowing and glorious fashion.

There's George Halas and his creation of the Chicago Bears. There's Curly Lambeau, who founded the Green Bay Packers. There's George Preston Marshall, first with the Boston Redskins and then in Washington. And there's Tim Mara with the New York Giants.

But no list of NFL "founding fathers" is truly complete without Bert Bell and what he meant to the formation and growth of the Philadelphia Eagles.

Bell's fingerprints are everywhere on the old—which became the modern—NFL.

"Dad took the NFL out of the dark ages and brought it into modern times," Bell's daughter, Jane, told *The Eagles Encyclopedia.*

Among his accomplishments are helping create the college draft, helping negotiate TV contracts, siding with the players in their desire to form a union, and settling a bidding war for players with the Canadian Football League. He is also reputed to have coined the phrase, "On any given Sunday," meaning any team is good enough to beat any other team depending on the week.

But in the early years, it was not pretty. The Eagles, formed from the wreckage of the disbanded Frankford Yellow Jackets, were not very good. In fact, they were awful.

In their first game in 1933, under the coaching eye of Lud Wray, the new Eagles were crushed 56–0 by the New York Giants. They played their first home game the following week under a set of portable lights at the Baker Bowl. With only 1,750 people watching, they fell 25–0 to the Portsmouth Spartans.

After another loss, this time to the Packers, the new guys didn't lose four in a row, lost two others, and finished the season 3–5–1, which includes a tie with the then-powerful Bears.

But the Eagles were not making much of a dent on the field or off. Indeed, by 1936, the franchise had lost more than $90,000 and was offered for sale at a public auction. The only bid was placed by Bell—for a scant $4,500.

Not only was he the team's sole owner. But that season, he also took over the coaching reins from his old friend Lud Wray, who had managed just a 9–21–1 record in three forgettable seasons. But Bell was more than that. Because times were tough, he also acted as team trainer, scout, publicist, ticket manager, and did anything else that needed to get done.

He would even drive the team bus, often driving his players into the country to find an open field that would prove to be a good place to practice. In those days, you did what you had to do to get the job done.

Bell was a good businessman and, in his day, was a pretty decent football player at Penn. He also coached at Penn from 1920 to 1928 and at Temple University in 1930–31. But when he took over the Eagles, he found pro football was a different animal.

In his first season, his team went 1–11 and scored just 51 points. Indeed, they were shut out six times, including four games in a row at one stretch.

Bert Bell, founder and head coach of the Philadelphia Eagles, talks to his squad on July 26, 1939.

It really never got much better for Bell on the sideline; in his five seasons, the Eagles won just 10 games.

By 1939 it became clear that Bell was not the answer the Eagles needed as head coach. But instead of a simple coaching change, Bell had something else in mind. It started with Art Rooney selling the Pittsburgh Steelers to Alexis Thompson and buying half of the Eagles with Bell.

In 1940, after another disastrous season, Bell/Rooney and Thompson traded franchises. Essentially, the entire Eagles organization—including most of the players—went to Pittsburgh, and the entire Steelers organization moved to Philadelphia. The cities

What's in a Name? How About Steagles?

In 1943 Pennsylvania's two NFL franchises were in dire straits. The Philadelphia Eagles were coming off a 2–9 season in 1942, and the Pittsburgh Steelers, since joining the league in 1933, had known just one winning season. Both franchises were struggling financially, and both had lost key players to World War II.

In an effort to keep both franchises afloat, NFL owners agreed that for the 1943 season, the Eagles and Steelers would merge into one team.

The team would officially be known as the Phil-Pitt Eagles-Steelers, but everyone called them the Steagles. They would play four home games at Philadelphia's Shibe Park and two at Pittsburgh's Forbes Field.

And the two head coaches—Philly's Greasy Neale and Pittsburgh's Walt Kiesling—shared duties, with Neale handling the offense and Kiesling the defense.

It sounded good in theory, but the two men, used to being in charge and being obeyed, butted heads constantly. One day during practice, Neale cursed a Steelers player who had made a mistake. Kiesling was so angry he took all of his Steelers players off the field in protest and didn't bring them back until the next day.

But while the coaches clashed, the players got along famously, cheering each other for just about anything. They understood the reality of the situation and reveled in it. They were having the time of their lives.

It was a pretty good team, too. The Steagles produced the NFL's top rushing attack, led by Jack Hinkle and quarterback Roy Zimmerman, whose only claim to fame was that he was the backup to Washington's Hall of Famer Sammy Baugh.

The merged team actually played well, posting a 5–4–1 record and finishing one game behind the Eastern Division–winning Washington Redskins and New York Giants.

In 1944 the two teams went their separate ways again—literally and figuratively. The Eagles, led by future Hall of Fame back Steve Van Buren and Hinkle, marched to a 7–1–2 record, their best ever. But the Steelers continued to struggle and had to merge again, this time with the Chicago Cardinals.

That team finished 0–10 and was derisively known as "the Carpets."

retained the team names in the switch, and the Thompson-owned Steelers became the Eagles. One of Thompson's first moves was to hire Earle "Greasy" Neale as Eagles head coach, and in 10 seasons, Neale helped the Eagles to their first sustained success.

In 1946, Bell took over as commissioner of the NFL and remained in that role until his death in 1959. Ironically, in the final days of is life, Bell had been negotiating to buy back his beloved Eagles franchise for his children.

It would have been a fitting ending to a remarkable life.

6 Doug Pederson

When Doug Pederson was named head coach of the Eagles in 2016, the reaction was practically universal.

Doug who? And perhaps more important, Doug why?

Who was this guy and why did the Eagles believe he had what it took to be a successful NFL coach?

One NFL insider, former Cleveland Browns general manager, 49ers scout, and Patriots assistant Michael Lombardi, said simply that Pederson "might be less qualified to coach a team than anyone I've ever seen in my 30-plus years in the NFL."

Ouch.

But Doug Pederson has heard, and seen, it all before, because nothing had ever really come easily for the affable, self-effacing Pederson, either as a player or a coach.

He had been in the trenches for years, bouncing around pro football for 14 seasons, never quite good enough to be a consistent starter but never bad enough to be forgotten. He was the quarterback teams looked to when they needed someone reliable to back up their starter in an emergency.

There were two stints with the Miami Dolphins, stops in the World Football League and the World League of American Football, disastrous seasons in Cleveland and Philadelphia, and, perhaps the most valuable, his two stops in Green Bay as Brett Favre's backup. He played for the Packers from 1995 to 1998 and again from 2001 to 2004 and he grew close to Favre. He often schooled Favre on defensive fronts and secondary coverages and he was approachable and helpful with the media, often answering questions in place of the increasingly reticent Favre.

He also learned how to coach, not only from watching head coach Mike Holmgren and later Mike Sherman, but from one of Holmgren's earliest disciples, Andy Reid.

It was through Reid that Pederson saw the best and worst of the game. He signed with Philly in 1999 in Reid's first season to be the Eagles' starting QB. It did not go well.

The Eagles struggled badly and Pederson was caught in the middle.

"The fans used to throw batteries at me," he said. "The big ones too. Those 'D' batteries. They threw beer at me. They spit on me. It was tough."

Pederson was eventually benched in favor of rookie Donovan McNabb and was released after the season. The next year he played in Cleveland, again as a backup, and was again released after the season.

He thought about retiring altogether but was lured back to Green Bay, where he stayed four more seasons behind Favre. He finally retired after the 2004 season and began his coaching career—with Calvary Baptist Academy in Shreveport, Louisiana.

In 2009, Reid called and Pederson moved to the NFL, first as offensive quality control director and then earning a promotion to quarterbacks coach in 2011.

When Reid was fired as Philly's head coach, Pederson joined his mentor in 2013 as offensive coordinator in Kansas City.

Even then, Reid knew his protege was ready to be a head coach.

"He's got everything he needs," Reid said. "He'll be a good one."

So when the Eagles hired him to replace Chip Kelly after the 2015 season, it seemed more an opportunity for the franchise to catch its breath after four years of Kelly's turbulence.

Soft-spoken, polite, and helpful, he was the antithesis of the brazen Kelly. But no one was really sure if he was ready for the job.

A 7–9 opening campaign did not inspire confidence, but in 2017, Pederson showed why he was the right coach. His analytical approach to the game was interesting enough but he was also a gambler, making the kinds of decisions during the game that surprised many, even his players.

He'd go for it on fourth down deep in his own territory because it felt tight. He'd call run plays in pass situation and vice versa because he had a feeling and, most important, he trusted his players. That feeling resonated throughout the franchise.

Nowhere was that more evident that in the Super Bowl and with the play which will be immortalized in the long history of that game. Late in the second quarter and facing fourth down on the Patriots 2-yard line, conventional wisdom said kick a field goal. It's what every other coach in the league likely would have done.

Not Pederson.

He called the play "Philly Special" and when the players in the huddle heard it, they all smiled. This was their coach at his best, doing his own thing and trusting his players.

Every Eagles fan can recall what happened. Quarterback Nick Foles went to the right side of the offensive line as if he were calling an audible. The ball was then snapped to running back Corey Clement, who lateraled to tight end Trey Burton, who was crossing behind him. Burton then lofted a pass to Foles, who was all alone in the end zone.

It was a bold, unexpected, remarkable call and it may well have cemented Pederson's reputation as a fearless play-caller—a great reputation to have.

Doug Pederson, the quarterback nobody wanted and the coach no one had confidence in, had stood toe to toe with the Patriots and their juggernaut and never blinked. Unafraid and unimpressed, he let his Eagles play with child-like abandon and it worked.

"You saw a terrific Doug Pederson," center John Kelce told fans during the Eagles raucous victory parade.

Even Michael Lombardi changed his view of Pederson.

"I was wrong," he said after the game. "This guy can coach."

His players always knew it.

7 Reggie White

Where to start with Reggie White? Likely the greatest defensive lineman in NFL history and certainly the best to ever wear a Philadelphia Eagles uniform, White could never be, and will never be, easily defined.

Brilliant at times, perplexing at others, he cared little for what people thought of him or the impression he left. He was a warrior on the football field who could perfectly justify the brutality of the game that made him famous and rich with the gentleness and understanding of his unyielding faith in God. An ordained minister, White always said he had a higher purpose in life than just rushing and crushing quarterbacks.

But oh, how he could rush the quarterback! With his fearsome and feared "club" move—where he'd use his right forearm and his incredible strength to simply knock an offensive lineman sideways—he remains the Eagles' all-time sack leader and is the second-best in NFL history. And while defensive ends will come and go, there will never be anyone like Reggie White.

But it wasn't always that way.

An All-American at the University of Tennessee, White was part of the fraternity of college players who took the staggering money offered by the upstart United States Football League, signing with the Memphis Showboats in 1984, where he posted 23½ sacks in 26 games.

When the USFL fell apart, the Eagles, who owned White's draft rights, signed him to a four-year, $1.85 million deal. He wasted no time paying dividends as he registered 13 sacks and was named NFL Defensive Rookie of the Year.

A new coach, defensive zealot Buddy Ryan, took over the next year, and that's when White truly began to flourish. Making White the cornerstone of his aggressive, attacking defense, Ryan turned him loose to cause havoc any way he could.

Over the course of eight seasons, White became beloved in Philadelphia—not exactly the easiest thing to accomplish. The chants of "REG-GIE! REG-GIE! REG-GIE!" reverberated around the old Vet and, in a very real sense, the mild minister from Chattanooga, Tennessee, became the face, heart, and soul of the tough old franchise.

With the Eagles, he became the league's most dominant pass rusher, period. He would require defensive coordinators to devise game plans solely for him, almost unheard of in the NFL at the time. Often two, sometimes three, blockers would be assigned to stop him, and White reveled in it.

In his eight seasons, White piled up more sacks (124) than games played (121), a mark that hasn't been approached since.

But by 1992, things were changing—not only with the Eagles but in the NFL. Philly had come close to NFL greatness under Ryan but had fallen short too often. Now Ryan was gone, and Rich Kotite was the coach…and a Super Bowl title—the only accolade White really sought—still eluded him.

By 1992 he was beginning to believe that, after eight incredible seasons with the Eagles, it might be time to move on. And in a November 1992 game at Milwaukee County Stadium against the Green Bay Packers, he had an inkling where he might go.

In that game, the Eagles mercilessly battered a young quarterback named Brett Favre. They sacked him twice, separating Favre's shoulder on of one them. Still, the kid showed the guts and the talent to rally the Packers to win.

"I always remembered that," White said. "He was beat up, and still he had enough left to win the game. I said to myself, 'This kid is special.'"

After the 1992 season, White declared himself a free agent, convinced that team owner Norman Braman would not spend the money required to bring in players that would lead the team to a title. That started a frenzy in the NFL never seen before or since. Everyone wanted White, but not everyone would meet the exorbitant price he was sure to command.

In Philadelphia, fans begged White to stay. A "Keep Reggie" rally at City Hall drew thousands and was the kind of civic outpouring few expected from Philly. But it was too late.

Despite being wooed by some of the league's top teams, such as Washington and San Francisco, White stunned the sports world by signing a then-inconceivable four-year, $17 million deal with the lowly Packers.

At the time, White said God directed him to Green Bay. Cynics dismissed that, saying this particular God was green and had a lot of zeroes behind it.

Whatever it was, White's departure to Green Bay changed the landscape dramatically. In Green Bay, White joined Favre to turn the Packers into an instant contender.

Four years later, White posted a Super Bowl–record three sacks as the Packers won Super Bowl XXXI. The enduring image is White sprinting the length of the New Orleans Superdome field afterward, holding the Lombardi Trophy high in his hands, photographers trailing him, grinning like a little kid.

That was the pinnacle.

After the 1998 season, White announced his retirement but changed his mind and signed with the Carolina Panthers in 2000. He retired again after that season.

White impacted two franchises forever—the Eagles and Packers. His No. 92 has been retired in both places (as well as at the University of Tennessee), and both cities claim him as their own.

Tragically, on December 26, 2004, White suffered a heart attack and died at age 43. Less than two years later, he was inducted into the Pro Football Hall of Fame, a full three years ahead of the usually required waiting period for election.

Chuck Bednarik

It was easy to look at Chuck Bednarik and his busted nose, shattered hands, and square jaw and think that he wasn't so much born as he was chiseled from some block of granite.

In his prime, he was the toughest man playing the world's toughest game. And there is no one who says "Philadelphia Eagles" more than Bednarik, born and bred and schooled in Pennsylvania.

He was raised in the tough steel-mill town of Bethlehem and forged, literally, by war. Indeed, at age 18 he enlisted in the air force and was the gunner on a B-24 bomber in Europe during World War II.

Upon his return, he enrolled at the University of Pennsylvania, where he was a two-time All-American and the first-round draft choice of the Eagles in 1949.

He quickly became one of the game's great 60-minute men, playing on both offense and defense because, well, that's what was called for at the time.

Throughout the 1950s he played center on offense and line-backer on defense, and he didn't just occupy the positions…he was a star at both. Indeed, even today he's still considered one of the best linebackers in NFL history.

But in 1959 Bednarik had seen enough and retired. The Eagles held a ceremony for their icon, presenting him with a color TV and a $1,000 check. At age 34, he had played enough, and he knew he had nothing left to prove.

Then again…

Early in 1960, Bednarik's wife had another baby, money was tight, and when the Eagles offered the kingly sum of $15,000 for him to play one more season, he jumped at it. The 1960 season would prove to be a season of fame and infamy for Bednarik.

Content just to play center, Bednarik helped trigger a terrific offense and watched as Philly took its place as perhaps the best team in the NFL. But in the fifth game of the season, against the Cleveland Browns, starting linebacker Bob Pellegrini broke his leg and was lost for the season. Uncomfortable with the rookie backup, head coach Buck Shaw turned to his old warhorse, Bednarik, to return to the position he knew so well.

"Defenses weren't as complicated then," Bednarik said with a shrug. "It wasn't that hard. The game is half instinct anyway."

What unfolded was a remarkable season that saw a 35-year-old veteran play both ways in an NFL where such things were becoming obsolete.

But for all that Bednarik accomplished in his career and, especially, in that 1960 season, he will always and forever be known for the play he made on New York Giants halfback Frank Gifford in a crucial game on November 20, 1960, at Yankee Stadium.

Battling a Giants team that was just a half-game behind Philly in the Eastern Division standings, the Eagles were hanging onto a 17–10 lead late in the game when the Giants began driving toward a tying touchdown.

Gifford, the Giants' top offensive player, caught a pass over the middle and was immediately clobbered by Bednarik. Gifford hit the ground, his head violently hitting the frozen turf. "It was a like a truck hitting a Volkswagen," Bednarik said later. "Frank never saw me coming."

Eagles cornerback Tom Brookshier saw, or more accurately heard, what happened. "It wasn't the usual *thud*," he said. "This was a loud *crack*, like an axe splitting a piece of wood. I saw Frank on the ground, and he looked like a corpse. I thought he was dead."

Not surprisingly, Gifford lost the ball and Eagles linebacker Chuck Weber fell on it, sealing the win for Philly.

What happened next has been argued for decades. In a *Sports Illustrated* photo, Bednarik is seen celebrating over the motionless Gifford. It was interpreted by many people as Bednarik celebrating the injury to Gifford. It is a claim Bednarik has vehemently denied for 50 years.

"I wasn't directing it to Frank or anyone else," he said. "I was just happy we won. If people think I was gloating over Frank, they're full of you know what."

Gifford suffered a serious concussion that ended his 1960 season and kept him out of the '61 season as well. And when he did return, one of the game's most graceful players was never the same. Gifford has time and again defended Bednarik for the hit and the reaction.

The Eagles steamed to a 10–2 season and faced the Green Bay Packers in the NFL Championship Game at Franklin Field. In that game, Bednarik was at his rugged best. He was on the field for 139 of 142 total plays, going to the sideline only for kickoffs.

But he saved his biggest play for the end, when the Packers, trailing 17–13 and poised at the Philly 22-yard line, had time for one more play. Unable to throw into the end zone, quarterback Bart Starr dumped a pass to his powerful fullback, Jim Taylor, who rolled over three Eagles defenders before running into Bednarik at the 9-yard line. Taylor went down and Bednarik, the wily veteran that he was, kept Taylor on the ground until the clock ran out.

"Now you can get up!" Bednarik barked at Taylor when the gun sounded. "This game's over."

That championship held particular significance for Bednarik, and not only because he had shunned retirement to return. "Man for man, we just weren't that good," he said later. "I still don't know how we won it, but we did."

Bednarik played two more seasons at center for the Eagles and then retired for good after the 1962 season. In 1967 he was inducted into the Pro Football Hall of Fame.

In the years since, he's had a hot-and-cold relationship with the team with which he is so identified, but he still revels in the years he played.

Asked a few years ago if he thought he could still play today, he laughed and said, "Hell yes I could play. I'd be a star."

But even forces of nature like the seemingly indestructible Bednarik don't last forever. In March 2015, Bednarik died at age 89, an Eagle forever and probably still convinced he could run down a fullback if he had to.

Said team owner Jeffrey Lurie after Bednarik's death: "He was a Hall of Famer, a champion, and an all-time Eagle."

Indeed he was. And always will be.

Steve Van Buren

When the Philadelphia Eagles selected a rugged halfback from LSU with their first pick in the 1944 draft, they could not have known what would follow.

The Eagles, after all, had not exactly lit up the NFL in their 11 years of existence. In fact, since joining the league in 1933, the Eagles had known only one winning season, and that was as a team named something else. The year before, as the Phil-Pitt Eagles-Steelers (or Steagles), the combined team had managed a 5–4–1 record.

Now, in 1944, the Eagles were back on their own, and their selection of Steve Van Buren with their first pick would be a prophetic choice.

It can be truly said that Steve Van Buren, a rock-hard 6'1", 210-pounder who was born on a fruit plantation in Honduras and went to college in Louisiana, was the Eagles' first superstar. Strong, fast, and humble to a fault, there was very little Van Buren couldn't do on the football field. It was no coincidence that after he joined the team, the Eagles finally became an NFL force, reaching the NFL Championship Game in three straight years (1947–1949) and winning it the last two.

Indeed, in Van Buren's career, which spanned from 1944 to 1951, the Eagles posted a 58–30–3 record and had just one losing season—Van Buren's injury-plagued final year in 1951.

"When Steve carried the ball, he struck fear in the heart of defenses," teammate Russ Craft said.

"Steve was the best runner in the game," said another teammate, George Savitsky. "He could run away from people but liked running over them better."

Known as "Wham Bam," "Supersonic Steve," "Blockbuster," and by other nicknames, Van Buren shunned all of them. He just liked to play.

Van Buren rushed for more than 1,000 yards twice, which in those days was no easy task. And in 1945 he grabbed the rare "triple crown," leading the league in rushing, scoring, and kickoff returns. He also saved some of his best performances for when they mattered most.

Perhaps nothing sums up Van Buren's self-effacement better than the 1948 title game set for Philly's Shibe Park against the Chicago Cardinals, to whom the Eagles had lost the title the year before.

Van Buren awoke the morning of the game and saw a blizzard raging. Assuming the game would be postponed, he went back to bed. But he decided he should at least make the effort to reach the ballpark and proceeded to take public transportation, then a trolley, and then walk seven blocks to the park for the game.

He ended up rushing for 98 yards and scored the game's only touchdown in a 7–0 win, the Eagles' first-ever NFL title. After the game, he walked the seven blocks alone again and repeated the same routine. The Eagles were back in the NFL Championship Game the following year, this time playing the Los Angeles Rams in a driving rainstorm at the Los Angeles Coliseum. It would prove to be van Buren's finest hour.

He rushed for what was a then–NFL Championship record 196 yards on 31 carries as the Eagles beat the Rams 14–0.

After the game, Clark Gable walked up to Van Buren, shook his hand, and called him the greatest athlete he had ever seen. After Gable departed, Van Buren smiled, turned to a teammate and said, "He seemed like a nice guy. Who is he?"

So it was with Van Buren.

That proved to be the high point for Van Buren and, at least in that incarnation, for the Eagles. Injuries plagued Van Buren in both 1950 (even though he still led the league in rushing attempts) and again in 1951.

Then at training camp in 1952, Van Buren suffered a gruesome knee injury that ended his career. He retired as the league's all-time leading rusher with 5,860 yards and held NFL records for most touchdowns in a season (18 in 1945) and rushing yards in a season (1,146 in 1949). Indeed, even today he still holds several team rushing records.

After his playing days, he tried coaching and scouting, but neither suited his personality. He was inducted into the Pro Football Hall of Fame in 1965 and also had his No. 15 retired by the Eagles.

He stepped away from football after that, moving to a quiet life in Lancaster, Pennsylvania, with his wife, Grace. There he ran an antique shop with his son-in-law and also owned a used-car dealership and a dance hall. He died of pneumonia in August 2012 at the age of 91.

10 Ron Jaworski

During his playing days, all Eagles fans had an opinion of Ron Jaworski.

To some, he was the epitome of what the Philadelphia Eagles were supposed to be. He was tough and competent. He worked hard, and he tried his best. He cared about winning, and he cared about doing it the right way. He was, in many respects, the classic overachiever.

To others, he was never able to win the games that mattered most. He made bad mistakes at the wrong times and, worse, he always seemed to make the same mistakes over and over. He quarterbacked an Eagles team that was on the cusp on being something truly special, and he was the wrong guy at the wrong time. He was, in many respects, the classic underachiever.

Every Eagles fan had, and still has, something to say about Jaworski—good or bad.

However, this much cannot be denied: whatever the Eagles were in the 10-year period from the mid-1970s to the mid-1980s when Ron "Jaws" Jaworski was under center, they were a more interesting team because of him.

After all, Jaworski was the quarterback that got the Eagles to the Super Bowl for the first time. With Jaworski at quarterback, Philly went to the playoffs four straight years.

By the same token, he was also the quarterback during a playoff drought when injury and inconsistency plagued him.

Still a fixture in Philadelphia and a familiar face on ESPN and *Monday Night Football*, no one understands better than Jaworski what a polarizing figure he was. But he also believes time heals all wounds.

"I might not have been the most revered athlete in Philadelphia history, but I think I earned the fans' respect," he said once. "I think they knew I gave it all I had every week. Win or lose, I was out there busting my butt."

And even his biggest detractors can't argue that point.

His career as a Philadelphia Eagle started quietly enough. Indeed, he is so tied to the Eagles and their history that there are many people who probably don't remember that he didn't end his career in Philadelphia.

He was originally a second-round draft pick for the Los Angeles Rams in 1973 after a record-setting college career at Youngstown State University. He joined a Rams team that had more than its share of quarterbacks—including John Hadl, Pat Haden, and James Harris—though none of them could take control of the starting position.

Jaworski was given his opportunity with the Rams, and he played well, including helping the Rams to a 1975 playoff win over the St. Louis Cardinals.

But after four seasons of turmoil in L.A., Jaworski wanted a new start, so after playing out his option in 1976, he was traded to the Eagles in exchange for All-Pro tight end Charle Young.

Ironically, the trade was technically illegal because neither Young nor Jaworski were under contract to the teams that traded them. But both men wanted out of their current situation so badly, no one made an issue of it.

Young ended up playing three frustrating, unremarkable years in Los Angeles while Jaworski flourished under Dick Vermeil, who was beginning his second season as Eagles head coach.

What Vermeil did with Jaworski was nothing short of sports-psychology genius. Plagued by uncertainty that led to bouts of inconsistency, Jaworski was told by his head coach that he was his starting quarterback, come hell or high water. "I knew he was the guy we could win with," Vermeil said.

Even during games when Jaworski was clearly struggling, Vermeil would pull him to the sideline and tell him he was in no danger of being pulled from the game. That positive reinforcement did wonders for Jaworski, and the result on the field was there for all to see.

After an unremarkable first season in 1977, where Jaws threw 18 TD passes and 21 interceptions and the Eagles won just five games, the pieces began to fall into place in 1978. The Eagles went 9–7, recording their first winning season since 1966, and reached the playoffs, where they fell 14–13 to the Atlanta Falcons.

But clearly, something positive was happening. The next season, Jaworski threw for more than 2,600 yards and 18 touchdowns, and Philadelphia ran up an 11–5 record and won a wild-card playoff game against Chicago before falling to Tampa Bay in the divisional round of the NFL playoffs.

In 1980 it all came together for Jaworski and the Eagles. The Eagles quarterback threw for 3,529 yards and 27 touchdowns, and Philly steamed to a 12–4 record and big wins in the playoffs over Minnesota and Dallas to secure the Eagles' first-ever trip to the Super Bowl.

While the Eagles lost Super Bowl XV to the Oakland Raiders, it was validation that Jaworski could be the quarterback he always thought he could be.

Unfortunately for the Eagles, the NFL's window of opportunity is small and closes quickly. Just two years later, Vermeil resigned after a 3–6 strike-shortened season, and it wasn't until 1988 that the Eagles had another winning season.

As for Jaworski, injures began to pile up and, after the 1986 season, with a young Randall Cunningham waiting in the wings to take over, Jaworski was released.

Convinced he could still play somewhere, Jaworski signed with the Miami Dolphins where, in two seasons, he saw limited playing time behind Dan Marino.

But in an emotional moment, the Dolphins visited the Eagles for a preseason game in August 1987. When Jaws stepped on the field to play in the second half, the Veterans Stadium crowd rose in appreciation. They had given him a brutal time in his 10 seasons as an Eagle, but they also remembered what he had done for them.

The standing ovation brought tears to Jaworski's eyes.

"I didn't expect that," he said simply.

In 1989 he signed with the Kansas City Chiefs, played a little, then retired.

He left as the Eagles all-time leader in pass attempts, completions, passing yards, interceptions, and touchdown passes. He also held the NFL record for consecutive starts by a quarterback (116 games), which started in 1977 and didn't end until he broke his leg in 1984. The mark has since been broken by Brett Favre and Peyton Manning, but the point was clear.

Jaworski, underappreciated as he was, was tough and resourceful and was a key reason why the Eagles enjoyed a successful five-year run.

11 Randall Cunningham

For a period of time in the NFL of the late 1980s and early 1990s, there was no more exciting player than Randall Cunningham.

He could do just about anything on a football field, and what he couldn't do, he would at least make an effort to do—often in spectacular fashion.

For a time, he redefined the quarterback position, coupling the ability to run with a great arm and turning the quarterback from simply a thrower to a multidimensional offensive force. He was Michael Vick before there was a Michael Vick.

In Cunningham's heyday, his coach, Buddy Ryan, would shake his head in amazement. "He's the best athlete to ever play the position," Ryan said. "He's got the best arm in the league. He's the best runner and the best punter. The only thing he can't do is play basketball."

Cunningham's star burned red-hot but relatively briefly, as injuries cut short what could have been a career for the ages.

He was a California kid who played college ball at the University of Nevada–Las Vegas, not exactly known as a college football mecca. Still, the Eagles were intrigued enough to take him in the second round of the 1985 draft. Their starter of eight years, Ron Jaworski, was approaching the end of his career, and plans had to be made for the future. And Cunningham could not have been a more different quarterback than what Eagles fans were used to.

Rolling into his first training camp in 1985, Cunningham oozed an arrogance that alienated some veteran players and even old-school coach Marion Campbell. It didn't help that when he did get a chance to play that first season, he didn't exactly shine, throwing eight interceptions in six games.

In 1986 Buddy Ryan replaced Campbell as coach and used an ill-fated quarterback-rotation system with Jaworksi and Cunningham that Ryan hoped would confuse defenses. It didn't. The thrower Jaworski and the scrambler Cunningham were sacked a total of 94 times that season.

Finally in 1987, the Eagles made the decision that the future lay in the legs and arm and head of Cunningham, and he responded with the kind of head-shaking plays that few could conceive of.

He would elude tacklers, glide past defenders, and deliver laser-like passes to receivers while on the run. He was, as he was later dubbed by *Sports Illustrated*, "the Ultimate Weapon."

By 1988 everyone knew about Randall Cunningham if for no other reason than for what he accomplished on one magical October night at Veterans Stadium. In front of a national TV audience on *Monday Night Football*, Cunningham made a play against the New York Giants that is still rerun time and time again—even in this age of instant information.

It was a third-down play from the Giants 4-yard line when Cunningham faked a handoff and rolled to his right, looking for an open receiver. At that point, Giants linebacker Carl Banks roared in and hit Cunningham just above the knees, seemingly knocking Cunningham off his feet and to the ground—like any other normal person.

Amazingly, Cunningham braced himself with his left hand, straightened up again, and drilled a scoring pass to tight end Jimmie Giles that helped spark a key Eagles victory.

"It was a play a lot of people would have gone down on, but I didn't give up," Cunningham said afterward.

The play was run and run and run again on TV, and everyone marveled at how incredible it was. But that was just Cunningham.

In four seasons, he not only led the Eagles in passing but was their leading rusher as well. Indeed, in 1990, he threw for 3,466 yards and 30 touchdowns (best in the NFC) but also rushed for 942 yards, the second-highest total ever for an NFL quarterback.

But for all his offensive pyrotechnics, Cunningham could not get the Eagles over the hump in the postseason. In 1988, 1989, and 1990, the Eagles reached the playoffs only to become a first-round victim each time.

Then, in the season opener in 1991, Cunningham suffered a disastrous knee injury against the Packers that ended his season almost before it had begun. He returned the following season to lead the Eagles back to the playoffs, but a broken leg in 1993 again ended a promising season.

By 1994, after a 7–2 start, the Eagles lost their next seven, and Rich Kotite was dismissed after four seasons as head coach. The team brought in new coach Ray Rhodes, who did not see Cunningham in his plans.

After a year out of football in 1996, Cunningham signed with the Minnesota Vikings and, two years later, he triggered the NFL's most prolific offense. At age 35, Cunningham was playing like a kid again, throwing for a career-high 34 touchdowns and earning NFL MVP honors. He led the Vikings to a 15–1 season that ended stunningly in an overtime loss to Atlanta in the NFC Championship Game.

After he was released by the Vikings in 1999, he played one season each for the Dallas Cowboys and Baltimore Ravens before retiring in 2001.

In 2004 Cunningham became an ordained Protestant minister and founded the Remnants Ministry in Las Vegas.

In his 16-year career, Cunningham threw for 29,997 yards and 207 touchdowns while rushing for another 4,928 yards.

It was a mercurial career that ended leaving fans wanting and hoping for more.

12 Andy Reid

Thanks to vagaries of time and history, Andy Reid's tenure as head coach of the Eagles will stand strong.

No, he didn't get the Eagles a Super Bowl victory in his 14 seasons, but his teams produced 224 wins and nine playoff appearances. When he was fired on December 31, 2012, after a 4–12 season, most agreed it was time to move on. But time will show he was the right coach at the right time and provided the franchise with an identity it desperately needed.

Ironically, Andy Reid, who was greeted with yawns and shrugs when he was named the Eagles' head coach in 1999, at least numbers wise, is the greatest coach in team history.

Reid was one of those coaches who picked the right time to strike while the iron was hot. He was part of the Green Bay Packers' staff hand-picked years earlier by coach Mike Holmgren. Of that original staff, four ended up becoming NFL head coaches, though Reid seemed the most unlikely of the bunch. But Holmgren knew years ago Reid would be a great head coach. "He absorbs everything," Holmgren said.

Reid served his tenure as an assistant at various levels, including in Green Bay, where he served as tight ends coach and, eventually, quarterbacks coach for Brett Favre.

By 1999, though, Holmgren had moved on to Seattle and Reid thought he was ready to take over a team of his own. There were a number of "hot" candidates available to replace the recently fired Ray Rhodes, but Reid made himself a candidate by sheer force of will.

Eagles owner Jeffrey Lurie remembers that Reid came to his interview with a six-inch-thick binder that included everything from his philosophy to how he'd run training to what players would wear on the team charter. And he brought a clear-eyed message about what the Philadelphia Eagles would need to be successful on the field.

Lurie was impressed. He knew Reid did not have the name recognition of some bigger-name candidates, but he also knew that big names don't always deliver the goods.

Trusting their instincts, Lurie and team president Joe Banner decided Reid was the perfect fit at the perfect time for the Eagles. Of course, his initial introduction to the dubious local media wasn't exactly awe-inspiring. Looking a little like a deer caught in headlights, Reid insisted he had a plan for where to take the Eagles but offered few specifics. "You have to trust me," he said at the time.

Few did. But as the years have rolled by, Reid has proven he can adapt as situations change. He swears he is the same guy he was when he first began coaching two decades ago. But he has changed.

And nowhere was that more clear than in the 2010 season when he traded his longtime starting quarterback Donovan McNabb with the intent of inserting Kevin Kolb as his new starter.

And Kolb did indeed start the season opener against Green Bay but was sidelined by a concussion. Michael Vick, the troubled rec-lamation project who was in is second season with the Eagles, took over and was brilliant, nearly pulling a late-game win.

Asked the next day who his starter would be, Reid confidently said Kolb. The next day, he changed his mind and named Vick as his starter for the rest of the season. "He just gives us too much for me to ignore that," Reid said.

Behind Vick, the Eagles reached the playoffs for the ninth time in Reid's 12 seasons. But, as happened so often, the Eagles could get no farther than the first round. And if there is a knock on Reid, that's it. He has a 10–9 playoff record, and four of those losses have come in the NFC Championship Game—and each of them to different teams.

Few question his game management and his ability to bond with players. But 12 years on one NFL team is a long time, and rumors surfaced after the 2010 season that the Eagles were thinking of replacing Reid with *Monday Night Football* commentator and a former coaching colleague of Reid's in Green Bay, Jon Gruden. Lurie quickly doused the speculation, but it was the first time Reid's job security was even questioned.

Indeed, Reid has spent so much time in Philly that he has formed his own "head coaching tree"—assistant coaches who got their start with him and became head coaches.

The list includes Brad Childress (Minnesota Vikings), Ron Rivera (Carolina Panthers), Pat Shurmur (Cleveland Browns), John Harbaugh (Baltimore Ravens), Leslie Frazier (Minnesota Vikings), and Steve Spagnuolo (St. Louis Rams).

In 2013, after he was released by the Eagles, Reid landed quickly as head coach of the Kansas City Chiefs, where he has produced playoffs appearances every year but one from 2013 to '17.

13 Donovan McNabb

It seems so long ago and faraway now. So many games gone by. So many passes thrown. So many triumphs recorded. So many disappointments recalled. So many what-ifs and never-weres considered.

It was, in short, one hell of a ride for Donovan McNabb as quarterback of the Philadelphia Eagles. For 11 seasons, he was the lightning rod for this franchise, and he accepted it all—good and bad—with a weary good humor that belied the uncertainty he felt inside.

Was he the best player in Eagles history? Probably not. He surely wanted to be and, in different circumstances, he might have made it. But between that infamous April day in 1999 when he was drafted and that stunning Easter morning in 2010 when he was dealt ignominiously to the Washington Redskins, he was the epicenter of everything that happened to the Eagles.

He was the guy who got the Eagles to five NFC Championship Games, but he was also the same guy who lost four of them. And in the one Super Bowl the Eagles did reach during his tenure, he was the quarterback who supposedly threw up in the huddle during the key final drive.

He could throw for big numbers but would also throw the interception at the worst time. Regardless, he was the face of the Eagles for a decade, but for too many people, that face said more about rampant underachievement.

Fair? Maybe not. But McNabb knew better than most what always befell NFL quarterbacks—too much credit in victory, too much blame in defeat. Such was life.

"I'm not a quitter, and I never give up," McNabb has said more than once. "No matter what kind of challenge I'm facing, I'm going to fight through it." And he's faced his share and always seemed to come out relatively unscathed on the other side.

It was never easy for McNabb. An athletically gifted kid from the Chicago suburbs, he led his high school team to the state championship but received only two college scholarship offers that would allow him to play quarterback—from Nebraska and Syracuse. He chose Syracuse and went on to a record-setting career.

When it came time for the NFL Draft in 1999, it was generally considered that McNabb and Kentucky's Tim Couch were the top quarterbacks coming out of college, while Heisman Trophy–winning running back Ricky Williams from Texas was the best overall player.

The new Cleveland Browns needed a quarterback and took Couch with the first selection.

The Eagles, under new head coach Andy Reid, had the second pick. In response, dozens of Eagles fans made the trip to New York City, the site of the draft, for what they assumed would be the selection of Williams and a new, exciting era.

Instead, the Eagles selected McNabb, and Eagles fans erupted in angry boos. Donovan McNabb? Another quarterback? What were they thinking?

McNabb came on to the stage for his introduction, and the boos continued to rain down on him. But McNabb kept his composure—at least on the surface. Underneath, though, he seethed with anger and confusion. "The dream comes true and they start booing," he told the *Philadelphia Daily News* at the time. "It was a shock. You try to forget the bad things that happen, but that was something I'll always remember because I'd never been booed before."

He made his first start for the Eagles in Week 10 of the 1999 season against the Washington Redskins, rushing for 49 yards, throwing for another 60 yards, and converting a pair of two-point conversions on the way to Philly's 35–28 win.

The Eagles stumbled in with a 5–11 record that season, but Reid already knew that McNabb was ready to take over as his quarterback in 2000. And McNabb flourished. He set club records (at least at that time) in pass attempts (569) and completions (330), while passing for 3,365 yards. He also threw for 21 touchdowns and was the leading rushing quarterback in the NFL with 629 yards and six touchdowns as the Eagles improved to 11–5 and won a first-round playoff game.

And while the boos were few and far between that season, expectations grew for McNabb and the Eagles. McNabb continued to pile up big numbers, taking his place as one of the NFL's top quarterbacks. But it wasn't until 2004 that he finally led the Eagles to the ultimate goal—Super Bowl XXXIX—where Philly fell to the New England Patriots despite McNabb's 357 passing yards.

McNabb was dogged after the game by rumors that he was physically ill during the final drive that came up short. Several teammates claimed McNabb was throwing up in the huddle and could not call several plays because of it. Also, as the seconds ticked away, the Eagles leisurely went to the line of scrimmage, showing no particular urgency to run a play. But Reid and McNabb vehemently denied the illness rumors and as for the slow pace of play, Reid said it was his decision.

Donovan McNabb (left) smiles as he stands on the sideline with head trainer Rick Burkholder during the final minutes of the Eagles' 38–14 win over the Arizona Cardinals in Philadelphia on November 17, 2002. McNabb suffered a broken right ankle during the first quarter of the game.

The Eagles never made it that far again under McNabb, and inconsistency and injury began to take their toll on the quarterback. In 2007, in the second round of the draft, the Eagles selected another quarterback, strong-armed Kevin Kolb from Houston, and for the first time McNabb began to think his days in Philadelphia might be numbered.

He did get the Eagles back to the playoffs in both 2008 and 2009, but they fell to the Arizona Cardinals and the Dallas Cowboys, respectively.

In the postmortem of that loss to Dallas, Reid insisted McNabb would return for his 12th season as the Eagles' quarterback, but behind the scenes the wheels were already turning.

Then, on April 1, in a stunning move, the Eagles dealt McNabb to the Washington Redskins for a second-round draft pick and two picks in 2011.

That McNabb, an Eagles mainstay, was dealt at all was surprising enough. That he was dealt to an NFC East foe was even more amazing. Those types of things simply aren't done.

McNabb handled the trade with grace and class but, again, deep down he burned. It was April 1999 all over again and, in a very real sense, he was being booed all over again.

McNabb departed the Eagles as the team's all-time leader in passing yards, pass attempts, completions, and touchdown passes.

But in the end, it wasn't enough.

14 Sonny Jurgensen

What might have been had Christian Adolph "Sonny" Jurgensen not been traded from the Eagles to the Washington Redskins? Who knows what direction the Eagles would have gone with the red-haired gunslinger? Who knows if he would have lived up to the considerable potential he showed in tantalizing flashes during his seven seasons in Philadelphia?

This much is clear, though. Today, Jurgensen is known as a Washington Redskin and went to the Pro Football Hall of Fame for what he accomplished mostly in Washington. And for longtime Eagles fans, they can't help but wonder, *What if?*

Jurgensen was a fourth-round Eagles draft pick in 1957 out of Duke University, a program that didn't throw the ball very much. But Duke's backfield coach, Hall of Famer Ace Parker, recommended Philly take the quarterback anyway, calling him, "the best pro prospect I've seen in years."

He wasn't big or especially athletic, even in those days, but Jurgensen could throw the ball with incredible accuracy. He would amaze teammates with his ability to throw the ball at any angle, while backpedaling, and while running in one direction and throwing another.

As a rookie in 1957, Jurgensen started four games and led the Eagles to two of their four victories that season, including a 17–7 upset of the powerful Cleveland Browns. In that game, Jurgensen threw one touchdown pass and scored another.

Coach Hugh Devore was fired after that season and was replaced by Buck Shaw, and almost immediately the Eagles made the decision to trade for veteran quarterback Norm Van Brocklin.

With his arrival, Jurgensen went to the sideline and watched for three seasons. "I had the chance to sit and study Van Brocklin, so I learned a lot," Jurgensen said.

In 1960 Van Brocklin guided the Eagles to the NFL championship and then retired, handing the keys back to Jurgensen.

"I knew I was ready," Jurgensen said. He proved it, too, having one of the best seasons an Eagles quarterback has ever enjoyed. In 1961 Jurgensen passed for a league-best 3,723 yards—a stunning number in those days—and 32 touchdowns. He had two 400-plus passing days and another three 300-yard passing performances.

The Eagles finished that season 10–4 and missed the playoffs a year after winning the NFL Championship Game. But the Eagles did compete in a meaningless postseason game called the Playoff Bowl, pitting the Eastern and Western Division runners-up. Philly was blasted by the Detroit Lions in that game, and Jurgensen suffered a right-shoulder injury that would plague him for the next two seasons.

In 1962 and 1963 the Eagles were simply awful, winning just five games, and the rage of Eagles fans fell to the logical place: the quarterback.

The criticism stung Jurgensen, so when new coach Joe Kuharich took over in 1964 and dealt Jurgensen and safety Jim Carr to the Redskins for quarterback Norm Snead and defensive back Claude Crabbe, he was relieved. No one needed a fresh start more than Jurgensen.

In Washington, Jurgensen was the unquestioned star. And even though he played on bad teams, Redskins fans were a lot more forgiving. He'd put up huge numbers but few wins, and he was still the toast of the D.C. area.

In 11 seasons in Washington, he threw for more than 22,000 yards and is still considered one of the greatest Redskins of all time.

Would he have reached that goal in Philadelphia? It's a question many people ask even today.

15 Norm Van Brocklin

He turned out to be the right guy at the right place at the right time for the right team.

With his vast experience and talent, Norm "the Dutchman" Van Brocklin took an Eagles team that had won only two games when he joined up in 1958 and, by the time he retired two years later, led it to an NFL championship.

"The Dutchman was the most unforgettable man I ever met in my football career," said wide receiver Tommy McDonald. "There wasn't a guy on our team who didn't think the world of him. He was a man's man."

Van Brocklin had already had a career and a half before arriving on the Eagles. He was a fourth-round draft choice of the Los Angeles Rams in 1949 and enjoyed the kind of success any quarterback would crave. Splitting time at quarterback with Bob Waterfield, Van Brocklin helped lead the Rams to the NFL title in 1951. That was the same season he threw for an NFL-record 541 yards against the New York Yanks.

He was a six-time Pro Bowler with the Rams, but he was also dissatisfied. Never had Van Brocklin gotten the opportunity to be "the guy" at quarterback. First he shared time with Waterfield and then he had to share with Bobby Wade. By the end of the 1957 season, he wanted a change and asked coach Sid Gillman for a trade. Asked where he wanted to go, Van Brocklin famously said, "Anywhere but Pittsburgh or Philadelphia."

And with good reason. The two Pennsylvania teams were NFL outposts, neither having won anything in years. In fact, since winning their last NFL title in 1949, the Eagles had dropped off the map, missing the playoffs each year, posting only three winning seasons, and coming off a 4–8 season in 1957 that led to the firing of coach Hugh Devore.

Nonetheless, Gillman dealt his cranky quarterback to the Eagles for a first-round draft pick, halfback Jimmy Harris, and tackle Buck Lansford. Already 32 years old, Van Brocklin seriously considered retirement until he spoke with NFL commissioner and Eagles founder Bert Bell.

In a deal that simply could not be made today, Bell promised Van Brocklin that if he joined the Eagles, he'd make sure he succeeded Buck Shaw as head coach when he retired. Van Brocklin agreed but never got anything in writing regarding the deal—an oversight that would cost him.

The Eagles remained awful in 1958, going just 2–9–1, but not because of Van Brocklin, who led the NFL by completing 198 of 374 passes for 2,409 yards. He also threw 15 touchdown passes and 20 interceptions.

They showed major improvement the next season with Van Brocklin throwing for another 2,600 yards. But during an October win over the Steelers, Bell suffered a heart attack and died in the stands.

Finally, it all came together. In 1960 Van Brocklin threw 24 touchdown passes and the Eagles posted a 10–2 record and beat the Packers in the NFL Championship Game, Philly's first championship in 11 seasons. Van Brocklin was named the league MVP and, in the locker room after the game, he announced his retirement.

When Shaw announced his retirement soon after, Van Brocklin thought everything was in place for him to take over as the Eagles' head coach, as Bell had promised. But with Bell gone and no document confirming the deal, Eagles management did not feel obliged to honor Bell's word.

He was asked if he'd assume the role of player/coach, but Van Brocklin immediately refused. Instead, he accepted the head-coaching job with a new NFL team—the Minnesota Vikings. He coached there six years with little success, then took over another struggling new franchise, the Atlanta Falcons, but did not fare any better. His career record as a head coach was 66–100–7.

After he was fired by the Falcons in 1974, he slipped away from the game for the most part and, in 1983, suffered a heart attack and died at the age of 57.

16 Dick Vermeil

For many football fans, Dick Vermeil is the name and face and voice for a term that has since found its way into the American lexicon: *burnout.*

But he was so much more than that.

For seven seasons, from 1976 to 1982, Vermeil not only brought the Eagles back to NFL relevancy but changed the mindset and attitude of a franchise that had no idea of where it was going or what it wanted to be.

He was teased for his emotions, often breaking down in tears during press conferences, and he was teased for the rah-rah atmosphere he brought to the team. But it all worked. "I thought he was Harry High School," veteran tackle Stan Walters said. "But he knew what he was doing."

Under Vermeil, the Eagles were 57–51 (including playoff games), they went to the playoffs four times, they won the NFC East division once, and they made it to their first Super Bowl. He was the first coach to leave his job with a winning record since Buck Shaw had departed 22 years earlier.

Vermeil had been ensconced in his native California as the head coach at UCLA. In Philly, Eagles owner Leonard Tose had just fired Mike McCormack, his third coach in five years, and he knew he needed to hit a home run with his next hire.

When talks with various coaches—including Norm Van Brocklin, Hank Stram, and Allie Sherman—came to nothing, Tose found himself watching the Rose Bowl on TV. In that game, a clearly outmatched UCLA team upset top-ranked and unbeaten Ohio State and Tose found himself attracted to the enthusiastic 39-year-old head coach.

"He lit up the screen," Eagles general manager Jim Murray recalled. "You could just feel his intensity."

Tose said simply, "Let's talk to that guy."

In February 1976 Vermeil agreed to the Herculean task of bringing the Eagles back from the dead. "I don't know if any coach in any sport ever took on a tougher challenge," Murray said.

Instilling his collegiate enthusiasm and armed, nearly daily, with another motivational phrase that would leave some veterans rolling their eyes, Vermeil attacked the job.

"We all had a sense we were moving in the right direction," linebacker Bill Bergey said.

But there was evidence to the contrary. In his first two seasons, Vermeil made little impact as the Eagles struggled to 4–10 and 5–9 records. But by the third year, with his players and his system firmly entrenched, the changes began. The Eagles posted a 9–7 record, finished second in the NFC East, and went to the playoffs for the first time since 1960.

The improvements continued in the next two seasons with the Eagles going 11–5 in 1979 and reaching the second round of the playoffs. For his work, Vermeil was named NFL Coach of the Year.

In 1980 the Eagles went 12–4 and easily won their division. They rolled through Minnesota and Dallas in the playoffs before falling to the Oakland Raiders in their first Super Bowl appearance. Vermeil was named NFL Coach of the Year again, and even jaded Eagles fans had grown to respect the job he'd done.

Dick Vermeil yells from the sideline as the Eagles play the St. Louis Cardinals in Philly on November 8, 1976.

When hired, Vermeil had talked about his five-year plan to get the Eagles back on top. With the Super Bowl appearance, it was five years. Then, almost on cue, things began to fall apart. The Eagles started the 1981 season at 9–2 but dropped four of their last five games and lost in the first round of the playoffs. Then came the strike-shortened 1982 season and, for the first time since 1977, Philly missed the playoffs altogether.

The long hours and the excruciating attention to details and the agony of losing was building up in Vermeil. In an all-night meeting with his family the night after the season ended, Vermeil broached the subject of quitting. Vermeil said it was his wife, Carol, who made the final call. "I said, 'I can't make the decision,'" Vermeil recalled. "Carol said, 'Well, if you can't, I can. We're getting out.'" Vermeil did not argue.

On January 10, 1983, Vermeil tearfully announced his resignation, saying simply, "I'm just burned out." It was that phrase many people focused on but, in truth, he said nothing other coaches who no longer had the drive anymore said. He had given everything he could for seven seasons, and there was nothing left.

Marion Campbell replaced Vermeil, but it wouldn't be until 1988 that the Eagles had another winning record and went back to the playoffs.

Vermeil stayed away from football for more than a decade, seemingly enjoying his role as a TV football analyst. But he was lured back in 1997 and in 1999 led the St. Louis Rams to their first Super Bowl title. He retired again but again came back in 2001 to take over the Kansas City Chiefs. He enjoyed some success but retired again after the 2005 season—this time, he said, for good.

He is now a motivational speaker and runs a winery in the Bay Area.

17 Tommy McDonald

Conventional wisdom, even in the NFL of the late 1950s, suggested Tommy McDonald never had a chance in pro football. Simply put, there wasn't much room for a guy who stood 5'9", weighed barely 170 pounds, wasn't all that fast and, for a receiver, had really small hands.

But this isn't the typical story of "little guy makes good"— even though he did. Even he had doubts about his ability to fit in and, though he had used remarks about his size as motivation to succeed, there was part of him that wondered if he really could make the cut. "I always had to prove myself," McDonald said once. "It wasn't until we won a championship that I finally felt I could sit down with the other guys on the team and feel no shame."

As it turned out, of course, McDonald didn't have to take a backseat to anyone.

A six-time Pro Bowler in his seven seasons with the Eagles, McDonald is still among team leaders in receptions (287), yards (5,499), and touchdowns (66). In the magical 1960 season, McDonald caught just 39 passes all season but 13 went for touchdowns, including a huge 35-yard catch for a score in the NFL Championship Game against the Packers. "If I had 11 Tommy McDonalds, I'd win a championship every year," Packers coach Vince Lombardi said afterward.

But what was it about this little guy from a small town in New Mexico who beat all the odds, played 12 years in the NFL for five teams, and was inducted into the Pro Football Hall of Fame in 1998?

"Tommy had more guts for a little guy," Eagles linebacker Chuck Bednarik said. "He'd catch the ball and would actually challenge guys. He'd run right at them. He'd take a big hit and he'd pop right back up and flip the ball to the official as if to say, 'Look, you can't hurt me.'"

Indeed, in his 12 seasons, McDonald missed only three games and, one time, after suffering a broken jaw, he had it wired shut and played the next week. He suffered several broken jaws in his career, mostly because he was one of the last players in the league to still play without a face mask. (He said it interfered with his ability to see the ball.)

McDonald was a third-round draft choice in 1957 though the Eagles weren't exactly sure what to do with him. They tried him first at halfback, then at defensive back, and then they had him return kickoffs and punts. Finally, late that season, the coaching staff decided to split him wide and make him a flanker. In his first game as a wide receiver, he caught two touchdown passes.

Quarterback Norm Van Brocklin showed up the next season, and the two men had instant chemistry on the field. Their first season together, McDonald only caught 29 passes but nine went for touchdowns. The next season, he caught 47—10 of those for touchdowns—and then came the 1960 season when he caught a touchdown pass, on average, with every fifth reception.

"That little bugger just knows how to get open," Van Brocklin said.

Van Brocklin retired after that season, and no one was sure what would happen with a new kid, Sonny Jurgensen, throwing the ball. McDonald joked with Jurgensen, telling him to just throw the ball to him and, "I'll make you just as great a passer as I made Van Brocklin."

He did too. Jurgensen threw for more than 3,700 yards and 32 touchdown passes, and McDonald had his best season statistically with 64 catches for a league-best 1,144 yards and 13 touchdowns, including setting a club record with 237 receiving yards in a game against the Giants.

He continued that consistency for the next two seasons. But when Nick Skorich was fired as head coach after the 1963 season, owner Jerry Wolman hired Joe Kuharich as head coach and general manager, and one of his first moves was to trade McDonald to the Dallas Cowboys for kicker Sam Baker, defensive tackle John Meyers, and offensive lineman Lynn Hoyem. McDonald, teammates, and Eagles fans were stunned. "I feel like I've been thrown away like an old shoe," McDonald said at the time.

He played one unhappy season in Dallas and then was dealt to the Los Angeles Rams, where he had a rebirth, going to his sixth Pro Bowl after catching 67 passes for more than 1,000 yards.

He played for two more teams, the Falcons and Browns, and retired after the 1968 season with 495 receptions, 8,410 yards, and an incredible 84 touchdowns, which, at the time, was second in NFL history behind Green Bay's Don Hutson.

McDonald moved away from football and concentrated on his oil-portrait business. Today, he lives in King of Prussia, Pennsylvania, and can often be seen at the huge mall there, walking and talking with shoppers.

After a 30-year wait, McDonald finally earned entrance into the Pro Football Hall of Fame, and no one appreciated it more. "There's only one place better than this," he said, "and that's heaven."

18 1960 NFL Championship Game

To this day, no one really knows how the 1960 Philadelphia Eagles won that championship.

It was a team that really did seem to materialize out of nowhere, offering little proof that it was a team to be reckoned with that season. Two years earlier, under first-year coach Buck Shaw, the Eagles were a miserable 2–9–1. The next season they were better, with a 7–5 record, good for a second-place finish. But in 1960, behind the magic of aging quarterback Norm Van Brocklin, the timely receiving of Tommy McDonald, and a bend-but-don't-break defense fronted by linebacker Chuck Bednarik, the Eagles somehow managed to get it done.

After opening the season with a loss, the Eagles proceeded to win nine straight, the team's longest winning streak, which wasn't equaled until 2003.

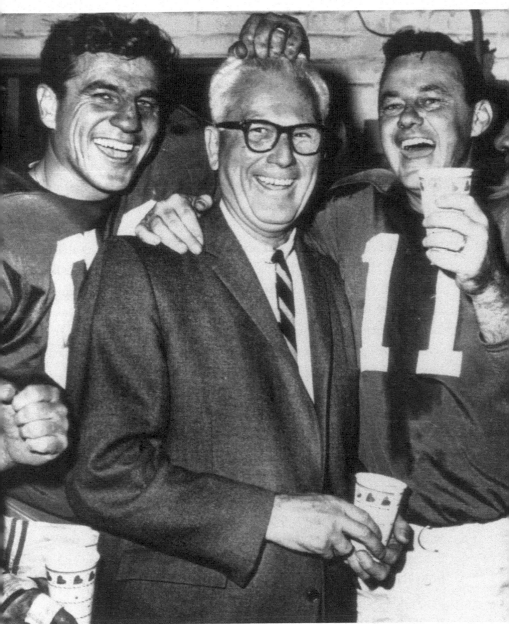

Eagles center/linebacker Chuck Bednarik (left) and quarterback Norm Van Brocklin (right) congratulate head coach Buck Shaw following the 1960 NFL Championship Game, a 17–13 Eagles victory over the Green Bay Packers on December 26, 1960.

The Eagles clinched their division with a December 4 win over St. Louis, then closed out the season with a loss to Pittsburgh and a win over Washington. With a 10–2 record, the Eagles were headed back to the championship game for the first time since they won their last title in 1949.

But this was no juggernaut. The leading rusher was a guy named Clarence Peaks. Ted Dean was an untested fullback, tight end Pete Retzlaff and McDonald were the best receivers, and Bednarik somehow kept the defense together and played center on offense.

The key to success was Van Brocklin.

"What Van Brocklin did with that team was unbelievable," said Sam Huff, the star linebacker of the New York Giants who lost to the Eagles twice that season. "They were strictly an average club. They had no running game, their offensive line was lousy, and their defense was mediocre. Van Brocklin carried them to the championship. With any other quarterback, that team would have been lucky to break even."

Perhaps, but the Eagles still found themselves hosting the NFL Championship Game on December 26 against the Green Bay Packers, who had finished 8–4, were coached by Vince Lombardi, and were on the verge of becoming the NFL's dominant team of the decade.

The Eagles took a 10–6 halftime lead, thanks in part to a 35-yard scoring pass from Van Brocklin to McDonald in the second quarter. It stayed that way until the fourth quarter, when the Packers moved in front 13–10 on a seven-yard touchdown pass from Bart Starr to Max McGee.

But then the Eagles did what they'd done all season—they took advantage of opportunities. Dean brought the next kickoff back 58 yards to the Packers 39. With just over five minutes to play, Dean swept into the end zone from five yards out to put the Eagles back in front 17–13.

Then came the real drama. The Packers got the ball back again with just over a minute to play and methodically marched the other way, gaining big chunks of yardage on the way to what seemed to be an inevitable game-winning touchdown.

The Packers faced a third down on the Eagles 22 in the waning seconds when Starr, unable to find a receiver in the end zone, dumped a pass to his tough 220-pound fullback, Jim Taylor.

Taylor plowed over three would-be tacklers until he ran into Bednarik.

The two men collided at the 9-yard line, and Bednarik wrestled Taylor to the Franklin Field turf and kept him there as he desperately tried to get up so the Packers could run one more play. The Eagles were world champs.

"That was the biggest tackle I ever made," Bednarik said.

"I never forgot that play," Taylor said years later. "That play was the difference between being a world champion and a loser."

In truth, the Packers outplayed the Eagles, rolling up 401 total yards to the Eagles' 296. But the Eagles also stuffed the Packers on two crucial fourth downs earlier and, of course, on the final play.

Van Brocklin didn't play all that well either, completing just nine of 20 passes with an interception and a touchdown. But he was named the game MVP, though it was Bednarik who deserved it.

In the locker room afterward, Lombardi told his team they would never, ever lose another championship game as long as he was coach. They didn't.

The Eagles did not return to an NFL championship until 1980 in Super Bowl XV. But the 1960 title game remains one for the ages and one that Eagles fans embrace more than the others because, in so many ways, it was so unexpected.

19 Super Bowl XV

In January 1981 the Super Bowl was taking root as one of the great events in America. It wasn't the two-week extravaganza that it would become soon enough, but by 1981, everyone was learning just how big a deal playing in the Super Bowl was.

And the Philadelphia Eagles were no different. That had always been their goal, to reach the Super Bowl. Coach Dick Vermeil had hammered that into their brains from the start of training camp, and it was the only goal that mattered: Get to the Super Bowl—and win it.

But no one could tell them what to do once they got there. No one could tell them how the atmosphere would be so unlike anything they had ever seen before. No one could tell them how to perform on a stage that was part Hollywood and part football. And no one could prepare them for the swagger, arrogance, and raw confidence of the Oakland Raiders.

"I just remember it all felt different," tackle Stan Walters said. And it was. No matter how they all tried to tell themselves it was a football game like a thousand others, they knew deep down it wasn't. There was the constant media attention, the stupid interviews that included the really stupid questions and, perhaps most important, the loss of the routine that was so important to all the players.

Football players, perhaps more than any other athletes, are creatures of habit. They practice at the same time. They hold meetings at the same time. They travel at the same time. They get to the locker room and change at the same time. Everything is rigorously timed on purpose to make things as simple as possible. The Super

Bowl was a complete change and, even today, players have trouble handling the shattering of their precious routines.

Looking back now, several Eagles players are convinced it was that loss of routine that cost them. "I don't think we were physically tired," linebacker Frank LeMaster said. "But we may have been emotionally drained. The week leading up to the game, all the hype and pressure kind of sapped us."

And then there were the Raiders. They had had a number of players who had played four years earlier in the Super Bowl, and they could tell the younger guys what was coming. Plus, dealing with turmoil was second nature for the franchise.

Owner Al Davis was in the middle of a battle with his long-time nemesis, NFL commissioner Pete Rozelle, over Davis' plan to try and move his team from Oakland to Los Angeles. In fact, Davis had moved the team to L.A. in the beginning of March 1980 before he was forced to move it back to Oakland at the end of the month.

Davis and Rozelle were in a pitched battle that was making its way through the courts by the time the Super Bowl arrived. The two men simply hated each other, and one of the great Super Bowl subplots was what Rozelle would do when handing the Lombardi Trophy to Davis if the Raiders won the Super Bowl.

But the Raiders were experts at putting the nonsense behind them—or perhaps feeding off it. "The relocations and legal actions were never allowed to become major distractions to our players and coaches," Raiders coach Tom Flores said. "Al Davis would never let these things be distractions. The main purpose was for us to win, and anything else was secondary."

To that end, the Raiders descended on New Orleans as though it was just another game, and their first destination, not surprisingly, was the French Quarter. The Eagles went straight from the airport to practice.

It set the tone for the week and, true or not, it was perceived that the Raiders were loose and confident and the Eagles were uptight and nervous.

Still, the Eagles were installed as 3½-point favorites, mostly based on the fact that they had beaten the Raiders 10–7 in an October game in Philadelphia where the defense had sacked Oakland quarterback Jim Plunkett eight times.

But the Raiders were more than glitz and swagger. They started the season 2–3 and lost quarterback Dan Pastorini for the season with a broken leg. In stepped 33-year-old Jim Plunkett, and he helped direct the Raiders to a wild-card playoff berth and then three road playoff victories against Houston, Cleveland, and San Diego, the last two on the road.

In the end, though, the Raiders' composure made the difference. Three plays into the game, Philly quarterback Ron Jaworski tried to thread a pass to tight end John Spagnola. Raiders linebacker Rod Martin intercepted the pass and returned it to the Eagles 30. Just a few plays later, Plunkett threw a two-yard touchdown pass to Cliff Branch and, barely four minutes into the game, the Eagles were down 7–0.

Jaworski later said it was the perfect example of Super Bowl nerves. "We ran that play a dozen times during the season, and I knew exactly what to do," he said. "It's an easy read. But you get in the Super Bowl, and you're all pumped up, and you think, *I'm gonna stick it in there*, and it costs you."

The problems continued when an apparent touchdown pass from Jaworski to Rodney Parker was called back on an Eagles penalty. And then came the backbreaker. Three plays later, after an Eagles punt, Plunkett stepped back and threw a pass that Kenny King gathered in at the 40 and took all the way, untouched, for an 80-yard touchdown.

The Raiders led 14–3 at the half, and the only dent the Eagles could make was a Jaworski-to–Keith Krepfle touchdown early in the fourth quarter to cut the lead to 24–10. But any hopes of a rally ended when Oakland moved methodically the other way and Chris Bahr kicked a field goal to produce the final score of 27–10.

"I think if we could have made a couple of big plays early, we would have been OK," Vermeil said afterward. "But we fell behind, and we seemed to sag emotionally. That happens in football. But give credit to the Raiders. They beat our butts."

The loss, evidently, was especially difficult for team owner Leonard Tose, who spent a fortune entertaining in New Orleans the week of the game. In a strange move, he even invited comedian Don Rickles to address the team before the game in an effort to lighten the mood. It didn't work.

Jaworski, the NFC's MVP, really didn't have bad numbers, completing 18 of 38 passes for 291 yards. But he threw three interceptions, all to Martin, and they were all costly.

"They tried going away from me," said Ted Hendricks, Oakland's other outside linebacker. "They went to Rod's side all day, and all they got for it was three interceptions."

Plunkett threw for 261 yards and three touchdowns and was the Super Bowl MVP.

As for the postgame trophy presentation, it was anticlimactic and actually rather civil between Rozelle and Davis. "You were magnificent," Rozelle said to his rival.

A year later, Davis completed his move to Los Angeles. In 1995, he returned to Oakland.

For the Eagles, the loss was a crushing end to a terrific season.

This was the fifth year of Vermeil's celebrated five-year plan to bring the Eagles back from oblivion, and he'd done it. The Eagles went 12–4 and won the NFC title by dominating the Dallas Cowboys in the division championship game. But they didn't complete the job. And the team would be changing. Stalwart middle linebacker Bill Bergey retired after the Super Bowl, and Jaworski never again had the kind of season he had in 1980.

The Eagles opened the 1981 season with a 6–0 record but lost six of their last 10 games and were beaten in a first-round wild-card playoff game by the New York Giants.

In the strike-ravaged 1982 season, the Eagles missed the play-offs altogether and, by the following season, Vermeil had quit.

It would be another 24 seasons before Eagles fans would soak in the surreal atmosphere that is the Super Bowl.

20 Super Bowl XXXIX

What image endures after the Philadelphia Eagles' 24–21 loss to the New England Patriots in Super Bowl XXXIX? Take your pick, really.

It could be the heroic effort of Terrell Owens, who caught nine passes for 122 yards on a leg that was literally put back together with screws. It could be Donovan McNabb's superb 357-yard performance against a Patriots defense geared to stop him. Maybe it was Brian Westbrook's 104 yards from scrimmage, showing again why he may have been the most valuable player in the NFL that year.

Or maybe it wasn't anything quite so noble. Maybe it was Owens' postgame tirade against the media. Maybe it was the criticism leveled at coach Andy Reid and his offense for the lack of urgency shown in the latter stages of a close game. Or maybe it was the infamous report that McNabb could not call plays in the huddle at the end because he was trying not to throw up.

Or maybe it was this: the Patriots won the game because they were the better team that was better prepared. The Eagles could have, and probably should have, won the game. They outgained the

Patriots on offense 369 yards to 331. They converted on more third downs, had more passing yards, and committed fewer penalties. But where it mattered most—precision, execution, and poise— New England ended up getting the better of the Eagles.

After seasons of close calls and near-misses, including defeats in the previous three NFC Championship Games, the Eagles had made the decision to do whatever it took to get over the hump. And that meant making a major splash in terms of bringing in the talent necessary to get the job done.

Many of the pieces were already in place, but Reid knew there were still components that needed to be added. So in March 2004 the Eagles completed the foundation of what they believed would be a Super Bowl team.

In early March, they signed free-agent defensive end Jevon Kearse from the Tennessee Titans, which immediately upgraded the pass rush. Then later in the month, the Eagles traded for Terrell Owens, the big-play wide receiver the Eagles had been seeking for years. With those additions; the return of defensive end Hugh Douglas and linebacker Jeremiah Trotter; and an offense that now featured McNabb, Westbrook, and Owens, the Eagles clearly believed they had the pieces in place.

And New York Giants coach Tom Coughlin couldn't disagree when he saw what the Eagles had assembled as that season began. "They're the standard now," Coughlin said. "Every other team now has to find ways to catch up."

But no one could. McNabb had his best season as a pro, Owens flourished in the offense, and Westbrook became a mismatch problem for every defense in the NFL. On defense, Kearse was as good as advertised (seven and a half sacks), a tough secondary led by Michael Lewis and Brian Dawkins stopped everything, and the Eagles led the NFC in scoring defense. It all resulted in a 13–3 record, which included losses in the last two games because Reid was resting many of his starters.

The Eagles rolled into the playoffs with McNabb playing the best football of his career—completing 64 percent of his passes for 3,875 yards, 31 touchdowns, and just eight interceptions. That made him the first quarterback in league history to throw at least 30 touchdowns and fewer than 10 interceptions. Westbrook ran for 812 yards and caught 73 passes for another 703 yards, and Owens caught 77 passes for 1,200 yards and 14 touchdowns.

But there was a dark cloud looming as the Eagles prepared to face the Minnesota Vikings in the division playoffs. Owens, who had been so spectacular all season, was out with a broken fibula and sprained ankle suffered in a December 19 win over the Cowboys. He would not compete in the playoffs, and his status for the Super Bowl, if the Eagles made it that far, was in serious question.

Still, the Eagles plowed ahead, rolling over the Vikings 27–14 and then finally winning an NFC Championship Game by over-whelming the Atlanta Falcons 27–10.

"It was a great feeling," Reid said in raucous Lincoln Financial Field after beating the Falcons. "With about two minutes left, the place erupted. The players felt it. I think it makes it even more worthwhile that we had to do it four times to get over the hump."

But get over it, they did, and now they faced a New England team that was slowly, steadily building an NFL dynasty. Led by coach Bill Belichick and quarterback Tom Brady, the Patriots could become just the second team in NFL history (next to the Dallas Cowboys) to win three Super Bowls in four years if they took care of the Eagles. What transpired on that February 6, 2005, evening at Alltel Stadium in Jacksonville, Florida, was a game that kept people talking for weeks.

The fireworks began even a few days earlier when it became clear that Owens, who had been declared all but out for the game because of his serious leg injury, had every intention of playing. The assembled media throng, many of whom were aware of

Owens' penchant for grandstanding, dismissed his pronouncement as Owens being Owens...again.

But there he was in pregame warmups and showing no ill effects of an injury that should have sidelined him for another month.

The Eagles were seven-point underdogs against the Patriots and, after a scoreless first quarter, the Eagles grabbed a 7–0 lead when McNabb hit tight end L.J. Smith for a six-yard touchdown. The score was set up on a beautiful 40-yard completion to wide receiver Todd Pinkston.

New England, who had sputtered most of the first half against the Eagles' swarming defense, finally got going late in the quarter, tying the game on a four-yard touchdown pass from Brady to David Givens.

The two teams exchanged third-quarter touchdowns—the Patriots scoring on a gimmick play when Brady threw a two-yard pass to Mike Vrabel (who was normally a linebacker) and Philly scoring on a 10-yard pass from McNabb to Westbrook. And, for the first time in its history, a Super Bowl went into the fourth quarter tied.

But it didn't stay that way for long. New England scored on the third play of the quarter when Corey Dillon blasted in for the touchdown from two yards out. Then, on the Pats' next possession, they made it a 24–14 game when Adam Vinatieri kicked a 22-yard field goal.

Then it got really interesting.

The Eagles got the ball back with 5:40 left to play and needing two scores. But instead of showing a sense of controlled urgency because they would need to get the ball back again, the Eagles operated as though it was the middle of the first quarter. They huddled on every play and walked to the line of scrimmage as though they had all the time in the world. It was a display that drew criticism from the TV announcers and fans everywhere.

The Eagles finally did score on a 30-yard pass from McNabb to Greg Lewis, but the casual approach left only 1:48 remaining in the game. And while the Eagles did get the ball back one more time (after an unsuccessful onside kick), there were only 46 seconds remaining, and they were on their own 4-yard line. The game ended with McNabb throwing his third interception.

Afterward, the main question was why the Eagles took so much time on that last scoring drive. Reid offered a nonanswer: "Well, we were trying to hurry up. It was just the way things worked out."

Tackle Jon Runyan tried to explain as well, saying, "If you get too hurry-up, you end up making mistakes. We had plenty of time."

But there was also the issue, brought up by a number of Eagles players afterward, that McNabb had been physically ill on that drive and couldn't call plays in the huddle. Hank Fraley said that McNabb was either so exhausted or so sick that he was vomiting and Mitchell actually had to call one of the plays because McNabb couldn't speak.

Also after the game, Owens, who had played so well and had been a model teammate all season, unleashed his frustration on the media, who had questioned his integrity.

Lost in the furor was the fact that the Eagles had come so close but, again, fell short. "Tough to take," McNabb said.

21 Terrell Owens

He only played in 21 games over two seasons for the Philadelphia Eagles, but Terrell Owens will never be forgotten—no matter how hard a lot of people might try.

He came to Philly in a whirlwind of optimism, controversy, and uncertainty, and he left much the same way, still convinced of his greatness and confused about why others never understood him the way he did himself.

"I just want to win" was always his mantra, and few doubted that's what he wanted. But his path to get there? Well, that was another story.

There was a time when Owens entered the NFL that many experts felt he had the skills to be one of the great receivers in league history. And while he put up impressive numbers, there was always something that kept him from being just a little bit better.

He was a third-round draft pick of the San Francisco 49ers in 1996 and learned at the knee of the game's best—Jerry Rice. In eight seasons with the 49ers, Owens caught 592 passes, and his 83 touchdowns were second only to the inimitable Rice in the franchise's annals.

But he had worn out his welcome in the Bay Area after constant clashes with the coaching staff and teammates, especially quarterback Jeff Garcia, who he was convinced would not throw him the ball on purpose.

Convinced a change of venue would benefit everyone, the 49ers allowed the free agent to look for a deal elsewhere after the 2003 season. The Eagles were intrigued because they had long needed a top-notch receiver to supplement quarterback Donovan McNabb. But coach Andy Reid was reluctant—he'd heard the stories and didn't need the kind of headaches he thought Owens would bring. But assistant coach Marty Mornhinweg, who had coached Owens in San Francisco, convinced Reid he was worth it.

Then came the first of the headaches. In an effort to get Owens' final years of his contract with the Niners voided, Owens' agent had to file specific paperwork that the 49ers organization insisted he had not filed. The Players Association and Owens appealed, and on March 4, 2004, the 49ers tried to trade Owens to the Baltimore

Terrell Owens hoists the trophy after the Eagles beat the Atlanta Falcons 27–10 to win the NFC Championship Game in Philadelphia on January 23, 2005.

Ravens for a second-round pick in that year's draft. But Owens refused to acknowledge the trade, saying he had become a free agent the day before the trade and had already worked out a deal with the Eagles.

Again, the NFLPA sided with Owens and, to avoid a major court battle, all sides agreed to a compromise. The Eagles signed Owens to a seven-year, $49 million deal, including a $10 million signing bonus, while the 49ers received a fifth-round pick and defensive end Brandon Whiting from Philly. The Ravens got their second selection back, and everyone was happy—for the time being.

Owens flourished with the Eagles. He and McNabb were on the same page from the beginning, and Owens caught three touchdown passes in the season opener against the Giants.

Through the first 14 games, Owens caught 77 passes for 1,200 yards and 14 touchdowns, breaking the club record of 13 last set by Mike Quick 21 years earlier.

Not only was he producing on the field, he became a fan favorite and a strong locker-room leader, not the cancer many people had expected. "He's given us an edge," linebacker Ike Reese said at the time.

With a top-notch quarterback in McNabb, a versatile running back in Brian Westbrook, and a field-stretching wide receiver in Owens, the Eagles seemed to have it all. And they proved it by running out to a 13–1 record. But, as is too often the case, the good times could not last.

After the Eagles' loss to the Patriots in Super Bowl XXXIX—a game in which Owens played superbly despite an injury that should have precluded him from playing at all—Owens tore into the media. Unfortunately for Owens, his postgame comments helped stamp out any second thought doubters might have had about him.

He was angry, sarcastic, and hostile. "The media made it look like I was grandstanding," he said. "In this situation, if it had been

Brett Favre, they would have called him a warrior." It was the beginning of the end of Terrell Owens' days as an Eagle.

In April 2005 Owens tried to renegotiate a new contract and was turned down by the Eagles. He threatened to stay away from training camp but did report, though he wasn't happy. Then it got worse. Prior to a game against the Cowboys, Owens said if he had it to do over, he would not have signed with the Eagles. He also criticized Eagles management and McNabb and enraged team-mates, fans, and coaches by wearing a jersey from former Cowboys great Michael Irvin while on the way to the team flight.

The next day, Owens and defensive end Hugh Douglas had a brief fight in the locker room and, finally, Reid had seen enough. He suspended Owens for four games. He never played for the Eagles again.

In March 2006, two years after he had arrived with such fanfare, Owens was released. Four days later, he was signed by the Cowboys. He played there three seasons before he again wore out his welcome and was released. He played one season with the Buffalo Bills and in July 2010, with no other options available, he joined the Cincinnati Bengals. In December of that season, he was placed on injured reserve for the first time in his 15-year career.

Never content to believe his career was over, he tried a stint in the Indoor Football League and had a brief, unsuccessful, tryout with the Seattle Seahawks. As late as 2015, he insisted he could still help an NFL team if just given the chance. But those opportunities never came.

He has kept himself busy simply being Terrell Owens, but while his antics seemed to overwhelm everything, his skill was never forgotten either. In February 2018, a humble and tearful TO was elected to the Pro Football Hall of Fame.

22 The Vet

Franklin Field had seen better days and the fact that the Eagles needed a new stadium was not news. But what kind they needed, where it would go, and who would pay for it were other issues. What they got was Veterans Stadium:"the Vet."

In some ways, Veterans Stadium was cursed from the beginning. It rose from argument, compromise, and uncertainty and, in the end, no one really got from it what they wanted. Still, it was the Eagles' home from 1971 to 2002, and there were plenty of memories—both good and bad.

The Vet was built in the grand scale of the time, a classic octagon shape that had been common for multipurpose stadiums of the late 1960s and early 1970s. Like other cities, the Eagles had to share the venue with the pro baseball team—in this case the Phillies—so the designs of all the parks looked remarkably similar. While proponents called the parks utilitarian, critics derisively called them "cookie-cutter" stadiums. And they weren't wrong.

But Veterans Stadium, named by the Philadelphia City Council, was the product of serious compromise from all parties involved, and while no one was completely happy, the Eagles were relieved to be out of Franklin Field.

But even the move wasn't without problem. The Eagles and Phillies had both expected to move into their new $52 million palace for the 1970 season. But labor problems, cost overruns, and bad weather pushed construction back, and the Eagles had to play one more season at Franklin Field. The Eagles front office was embarrassed and furious.

Finally the stadium was ready in 1971. Then again, it really wasn't. Eagles general manager Pete Retzlaff walked the field prior to the first game and was appalled by what he saw. Because the field had to convert to baseball, there were seams, holes, and divots all around the surface. The AstroTurf was laid down on a cement surface and provided no cushion for players. "It makes me sick to look at it," Reztlaff said.

But there was little that could be done at that stage. This much is clear: more than a few careers were damaged or ended altogether by the awful turf that became a laughingstock over the years. Perhaps the most memorable and gruesome accident came in 1993 when Chicago Bears wide receiver Wendell Davis ruptured the

The 700 Level

It was affectionately—or maybe not—known as the "Nest of Death," and a certain cross-section of Eagles fans loved it.

Also known by the more pedestrian "700 Level," it was where many felt the "real" Eagles fans hung out. It was also a place where you didn't go unless you knew what to expect. Drunkenness, public urination, vile language, a fistfight every now and then—that was the reputation of the 700 Level, which was located high in the upper deck of the circular stadium.

"It was a good baptism for going to the Vet," said a longtime season-ticket holder who got his start at the 700 Level then moved when he got a chance. "You never take kids up there. Never."

In his book, *If Football's a Religion, Why Don't We Have a Prayer?*, longtime Philadelphia journalist Jere Longman referred to the 700 Level as a place for "hostile taunting, fighting, public urination and general strangeness."

But those who resided there say it was all overblown. "The 700 Level is very unique," one longtime season-ticket holder told the *Washington Times.* "It's a place some people fear and others are proud to sit in. We just try to put the fear of God in people."

When the Vet was destroyed, so too was the legend of the 700 Level. In the Eagles' new home at the Linc, officials made a point of ensuring nothing like that evolved again, and so far it hasn't.

patellar tendons on both knees when he turned wrong on the turf. He never played again.

A 2001 preseason game with the Baltimore Ravens was cancelled because the field was in such bad shape. "We've been going through this for years," Eagles president Joe Banner said. "The conditions this team is forced to play in are absolutely unacceptable and an embarrassment to the city of Philadelphia."

Banner could say that knowing that three months earlier construction had begun on the new ballpark that would be known as Lincoln Financial Field. Still, it was another black eye.

Finally, the end came for the Vet. And while many people were glad to see it abandoned, many others held fond memories. After all, it was home to a lot Eagles football and, for many fans and players, it was the only stadium they knew. "I'm sure a lot of guys are going to say they won't miss the Vet," Eagles defensive end Hugh Douglas said. "But that's what Philadelphia is known for. When a lot of people think about Philadelphia, they think about football and they think about the Vet."

In March 2004 the Vet was imploded in a record 64 seconds. In September 2005, the second anniversary of the stadium's final game, a historical marker commemorating where the stadium once stood was dedicated and, in April 2006, more markers were erected to point out where home plate, the pitcher's mound, and the goal posts had once stood.

The Vet was gone but not quite forgotten.

Ralph Goldston

For Ralph Goldston, it was a chance to play professional football. For everyone else? Well, that was their problem.

He was no trailblazer, and he was certainly no breaker of barriers—at least not on purpose. All he wanted was a chance in the NFL, and the Philadelphia Eagles gave him that chance in 1952. That he was the first African-American to ever suit up for the franchise made no difference to him. He said that then, and he said it forever after as well.

"I didn't know about any color line," he said as recently as 2005. "I didn't find out I was the first black player until I was there a while. It wasn't a big deal." By that stage, it probably wasn't. After all, the NFL had been integrated since 1946 and Major League Baseball followed suit, finally, in 1947 with the signing of Jackie Robinson.

So when the Eagles drafted Goldston, a running back from Youngstown (Ohio) State, in the 11th round and then Don Stevens, a running back from Illinois, in the 30th round, it didn't cause a major stir. Keep in mind that the NFL was not completely integrated until 1962 when the Washington Redskins, the last holdout, signed Bobby Mitchell.

The Eagles drafted both Goldston and Stevens not to make a statement about civil rights but to get better in the backfield. Their best back, Steve Van Buren, was wearing down, and they needed to improve their running game quickly.

Ironically, while neither Goldston nor Stevens cared much about the race issue, the Eagles' first-round pick that season, African-American running back Johnny Bright, did.

The Eagles had hoped to feature Bright in the backfield, but before they got the chance, Bright opted to sign with the Canadian Football League because he said he did not want to be the Eagles' first black player. "There was a tremendous influx of Southern players into the NFL, and I didn't know what kind of treatment I could expect," he said later.

And as members of the Eagles, both Goldston and Stevens did see racism firsthand. On road trips, both men usually had to stay at a different hotel than their teammates, but Goldston just shrugged it off. "It just meant Don and I didn't have curfew," he said.

Goldston played four seasons for the Eagles but never quite found his niche. Though he started as a running back, he was slowed by a broken leg in 1953 and was shifted to defensive back in 1954. Stevens' career never really got off the ground.

In 1956 Eagles coach Jim Trimble, who had lobbied so hard to draft Goldston, was hired to coach the Hamilton Tiger-Cats of the CFL and Goldston, who had just been released by the Eagles, came with him.

In Canada, Goldston enjoyed a solid 10-year career in which he played both wide receiver and defensive back. After retiring, he coached in the CFL and in the college ranks. He passed away on July 9, 2011, at the age of 82.

24 Harold Carmichael

He still stands tall—literally and figuratively. His numbers have survived the years and the evolution of the NFL into a passing league, and Harold Carmichael remains the Eagles' all-time leading receiver nearly 30 years after leaving the team.

Consider these numbers: he is the team's all-time leader in receptions (589), touchdown receptions (79), and games played (180), and he remains one of the NFL's best in consecutive games with a reception (127). And all this from a guy who no one could figure out what to do with during the first two years of his career.

In 1971 Carmichael was an anomaly—a 6'8" wide receiver. No one had seen anything like that before, and many teams were certain with his slight frame (he was just 225 pounds), he might well be broken in two in the NFL. But the Eagles took a chance, drafting him in the seventh round. It proved to be one of the great steals in Eagles draft history.

Though a wide receiver in college, the Eagles moved him to tight end as a rookie and, before he could develop, his season ended with a devastating knee injury. The next season, he still wasn't showing much and, for his first two seasons, he had only 40 receptions.

But it was in the 1973, when Mike McCormack took over as head coach, when everything changed for Carmichael. McCormack had the simple but brilliant idea to let the kid who thrived as a wide receiver in college become a wide receiver again. He liked the idea of a 6'8" wide receiver being able to create stunning mismatches with shorter defensive backs. And it worked. That season, he snagged 67 passes and never caught fewer than 42 passes a season in the next nine years. And most of this was done in a 14-game schedule.

But while McCormack was credited for putting him in the right position, it was with Dick Vermeil where Carmichael really flourished. In the late 1970s, he became the league's most dangerous receiver not only because of his size but due to his precise route running and uncanny ability to find the end zone.

In 1978 he averaged nearly 20 yards per reception, a stunning figure in those days, and scored eight touchdowns. In 1979 he scored 11 more touchdowns and his ability to catch passes, sometimes off the top of a defender's helmet, became legendary.

Later, Carmichael admitted he wasn't a big fan of having to catch those high passes. "I might catch it once or twice, but one of those times I'm going to be up in the air and somebody's going to get a good shot on me," he said.

And quarterback Ron Jaworski made it clear that Carmichael was more than just a tall target. "Harold was never given the credit for being the great athlete that he was," he said. "People say, 'He's 6'8", just throw it up there and he'll get it.' But it wasn't just that. He ran great patterns. He had good hands. He caught a lot of passes down around his ankle."

Carmichael's production began to tail off in 1982 and 1983, and after that 1983 season, the Eagles released their all-time leading receiver. Amazingly, he signed with the hated rival Dallas Cowboys and spent a miserable season on the bench. He retired after the 1984 season.

"The truth is I didn't even want to go down there," he said later. "That Eagles-Cowboys rivalry runs deep. I'll always be an Eagle."

And he still is. In 1998, he rejoined the team as director of player development and alumni relations and in 2014 was named to the role of Fan Engagement Liaison. He retired a year later but remains a visible and vocal ambassador for the team.

25 Miracle at the Meadowlands

It was over, and everyone knew it.

The fans at the Meadowlands, knowing their New York Giants had beaten the Philadelphia Eagles, got out of their seats and headed to the exits for the long trip home. The TV announcers covering the game started to thank all the personnel who had helped with the broadcast. Eagles cornerback Herman Edwards found Giants running back Doug Kotar and said, "OK, man, we'll see you in a couple of weeks back in Philly." Kotar said simply, "OK, see you then."

It was over, and everyone knew it.

Except, of course, it wasn't, and what happened next still resonates through the NFL even today.

It was November 19, 1978, the day of the "Miracle at the Meadowlands," and those players involved still shake their heads in amazement and those fans who saw it still cannot believe it. But it's a play every football fan has seen a thousand times. It has been replayed and analyzed, and all these years later, it still doesn't make any sense.

The simple storyline? Well, there really isn't one. The Giants led the Eagles 17–12, and they had the ball with 30 seconds to play. All the Giants needed to do was kneel down with the ball, and the game would be over.

But incredibly, quarterback Joe Pisarcik tried to hand the ball to fullback Larry Csonka. The ball hit Csonka on the hip, fell to the ground, and bounced perfectly into Herman Edwards' waiting arms. He took the ball back 26 yards for perhaps the most improbable touchdown in NFL history. "Unbelievable," Edwards says even today.

That's the abridged version. But there are many more twists and turns to this story of one of the NFL's most notorious plays.

In 1978 the Eagles were a team on the verge of something special. In the third season under Dick Vermeil, the pieces were in place to get Philly back to the playoffs for the first time since their last NFL title in 1960.

They went to the Meadowlands with a 6–5 record and clinging to a wild-card playoff berth. A win over the 5–6 Giants was crucial if the Eagles wanted to maintain that advantage. But they played poorly, and Pisarcik took advantage, throwing two touchdown passes. Meanwhile, the Eagles failed to convert on two crucial extra points and trailed 17–12 late in the fourth quarter.

But the Eagles got new life when Kotar fumbled. Had the Eagles made their extra point, a field goal would have at least tied the game, but instead the Eagles had to try and score a touchdown. The result was a Ron Jaworski interception that all but ended the game.

But this is where it really got interesting. After a running play on first down, Pisarcik followed generally accepted wisdom on second down by taking the snap and kneeling down. But on that play, Eagles middle linebacker Bill Bergey smashed into Giants center Jim Clack, driving him back into the prone Pisarcik.

Not wanting to expose his quarterback to any more punishment, Giants offensive coordinator Bob Gibson made a fateful decision. Besides wanting to protect his quarterback, Gibson hated the concept of the kneel-down, believing it was unsportsmanlike. So he called 65 Power-Up, a handoff to the veteran Csonka.

When Pisarcik called the play in the huddle, the Giants were stunned. Csonka told Pisarcik to change the play, but the quarterback had been warned weeks before by Gibson never to change one of his play calls. So he went ahead with it. Csonka said he wouldn't take the ball if handed to him, but Pisarcik claimed he never heard him say that.

The snap from Clack surprised Pisarcik, and he barely had control of the ball when he tried to feed it to Csonka. The ball hit the fullback on the right hip, and that's when Edwards picked it up and ran it in for the touchdown. The stadium was silent except for the celebration by the disbelieving Eagles.

"I don't remember anything until I got into the end zone," Edwards said.

The win propelled the Eagles forward and they eventually secured their first playoff berth in 18 seasons with a 9–7 record.

The Giants? Gibson was fired the next day and head coach John McVay was relieved of his duties after the season. Gibson never coached again and never did talk about what happened that cold afternoon in New Jersey.

That play also fundamentally changed how teams approached end-of-game situations. Today, it's part of a team's playbook to have a "victory" formation in the final seconds of a game they're winning: two players right behind the quarterback and a third 10 yards behind the line of scrimmage—just in case. No team ever wants to feel the way the Giants did in the closing seconds against the Eagles.

As for what happened, there are still no real answers.

"I think it was just fate," Edwards said.

That's as good an answer as any other.

26 Buddy Ryan

He was the epitome of the phrase, "What you see is what you get." Buddy Ryan was all that and more.

He was profane, funny, and completely unconcerned with what people thought of him. He had made his reputation as a brilliant defensive tactician, and he wanted everyone to know how good he was and often enjoyed his critics more than his supporters.

While he tried to perpetuate his image as a down-home hayseed who taught football by the seat of his pants, there was a method to his madness, and it translated to his players.

Ryan had paid his dues in the coaching ranks, working his way from Texas high school football to the college ranks at places like Vanderbilt and Pacific and then to the NFL, where he was an assistant with the New York Jets and Minnesota Vikings before joining the Chicago Bears as defensive coordinator in 1978. That's where the legend of Buddy Ryan truly took root.

He developed the vaunted, feared, and much-misunderstood "46" defense and by 1984 had perfected it. His defenses swarmed and intimidated and then would tell anyone who would listen all about it.

In 1985 the Bears reached the pinnacle, playing the kind of defense most teams could only imagine, rolling to a 15–1 record and then cruising to the Super Bowl title. That off-season, Eagles owner Norman Braman read a *New York Times* article about how Ryan had constructed the Bears defense. He decided then he had to have him for his head coach, even though Ryan had not been a head coach of anything since his days in high school 25 years earlier. Nonetheless, Ryan, whose relationship with Bears head coach Mike Ditka had deteriorated badly, took the opportunity and ran with it.

In 1986 Ryan took over an Eagles team that hadn't had a winning season since 1981. The Eagles' reputation had suffered since the halcyon days of Dick Vermeil—they were predictable, bad and, perhaps worst of all, boring.

Years later, Ryan confided that, "Anybody who knew a damn thing about football knew we didn't have a chance in 1986." And he was right. Those Eagles finished 5–10–1, but Ryan brought a new attitude, a swagger and confidence that they probably didn't deserve.

But that was part of "Buddyball." He would remake the defense in the image of what he did in Chicago. It would be a hard-hitting, nasty bunch that wanted to send a message: we may not win all our games, but we're going to make you remember who you played. "We bring young kids in here who are cocky and arrogant," Ryan said at the time. "They believe in themselves."

Ryan didn't care who he offended, including team owner Braman. And in 1987, when the NFLPA striked and walked out for three games, Ryan backed the veteran players. When replacement players were brought in by the owners, Ryan refused to coach them, standing in the background watching silently. And he never did anything silently.

He also told the veteran players to stick together and not cross the picket line. That stance endeared him to the players Ryan wanted to coach in the first place.

Philly lost all three replacement games, damaging any hopes of the playoffs as the Eagles finished 7–8.

Finally in 1988 the Eagles got over the hump, winning six of their last seven games, posting a 10–6 record and capturing the NFC East title. Despite losing to the Bears in the first round of the playoffs, everyone believed the Eagles were on the right track. Ryan

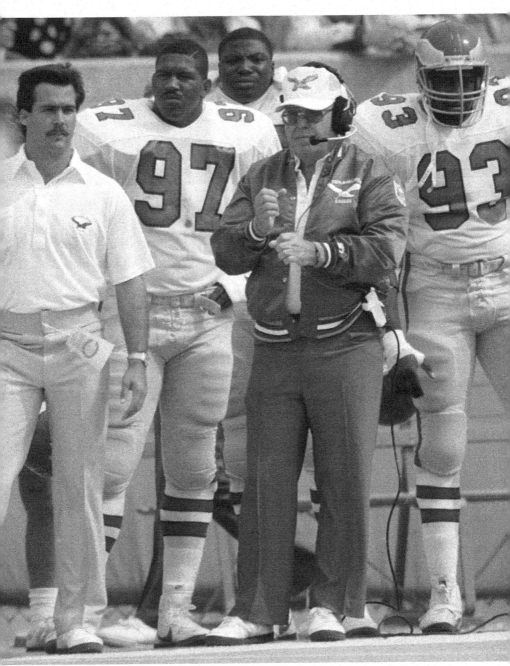

Eagles coach Buddy Ryan works the sideline during a game against the Bears in Chicago on September 14, 1986. Ryan brought the same brutal and brilliant defense to the Eagles that he had cultivated with the Bears years before.

had created a fearsome defense and now just needed the offense to catch up.

In 1989 the Eagles went 11–5 but finished second to the New York Giants in the division and again lost in the first round of the playoffs, this time to the Los Angeles Rams. Ryan had gotten the Eagles to a certain level but had taken them no further, and grumblings were starting to be heard.

In 1990 the Eagles led the NFL in penalties and penalty yardage, and rumors circulated that Ryan was paying "bounties" to

The Body Bag Game

One of the byproducts of any Buddy Ryan–coached team is a ferocious defense that can send grown men screaming into the night.

An example of that was a November 12, 1990, game at the Vet against the Washington Redskins. As with many stories in the NFL, what happened usually depends on who you talk to. From one perspective, the Eagles played dirty and deliberately knocked six Redskins from the game with serious injuries. On the other side, they simply played tough football and it was bad luck what happened. The truth? It was probably somewhere in the middle.

In the end, six Redskins were knocked out of the game, including two quarterbacks—Jeff Rutledge (broken thumb) and Stan Humphries (sprained knee)—and two kick returners in Walter Stanley (sprained knee) and Joe Howard (concussion).

As the carnage built up, Eagles defensive back William Frizzell walked by the Redskins bench and asked, "You need any more body bags?" The statement outraged the Redskins and delighted Eagles fans, who reveled in their team's tough-guy image. Almost immediately, the game was coined "the Body Bag Game."

Though the Eagles denied there was a deliberate intent to hurt anyone, that game continued to build on the Eagles' growing reputation as the dark empire of the NFL.

But the Redskins got their share of revenge. Almost two months later, in the first round of the playoffs, the Redskins went back to Philadelphia and handed the Eagles a tough loss that spelled the end of the Buddy Ryan regime.

his defenders for deliberately injuring opposing players. Ryan and his players denied it, but the image of the Eagles as out-of-control renegades grew.

In 1990, when the Eagles went 10–6 but were again ousted from the playoffs in the opening round, Braman had seen enough. The Eagles' image was taking a hit, Ryan showed nothing but disdain for the front office, and there was no sign of improvement on the field. So he was fired after that season. "I've been fired before for losing," Ryan recalled later. "But I've never been fired for winning."

But the Buddy Ryan Show was far from over. Two years later, he was named defensive coordinator of the Houston Oilers, where he famously took a swing at offensive coordinator Kevin Gilbride during a game. In 1994 he got another head-coaching gig with the Arizona Cardinals, where he won just 12 games in two years and was fired after the 1995 season.

Ryan retired from the spotlight after that and his final years were difficult. He suffered from Alzheimer's disease as well as cancer and also suffered a stroke, which left him barely able to communicate. Yet many of his former players, especially from the Bears, would make pilgrimages down to his Kentucky farm to remember those days long ago. Ryan died in 2016.

27 Pete Pihos

He may have been the first great tight end in NFL history. A rock-solid 6'1" and 215 pounds, Pete Pihos—nicknamed "the Golden Greek"—always proudly said he never dropped a pass in his nine-year career with the Eagles.

Tough and rugged, he could get open anywhere on the field and no one would take a ball away from him when it was headed in his direction. His 373 career receptions remain fourth all-time in team history, and he was a six-time Pro Bowler from 1950 to 1955. Only Chuck Bednarik (eight) and Reggie White (seven) went more times as Eagles.

"There was nothing he couldn't do," said his coach and close friend Jim Trimble.

He was already a star in college where, at Indiana University, he was only the second player collegiately to be named an All-American at two different positions (the other was Bronko Nagurski). In Pihos' case, he was a standout at fullback and end.

The Eagles drafted Pihos in the fifth round of the 1945 draft even though they already knew, due to his military service, he wouldn't be available until the 1947 season. "I can wait for a player like Pihos," coach Greasy Neale said at the time.

Pihos served 14 months in World War II, was part of the D-Day invasion, and served under General George Patton, where he earned five combat medals and a battlefield commission. So competing in the NFL? That was no big deal.

As predicted, when Pihos did join the Eagles in 1947, he was a force to be reckoned with. He missed only one game in his nine seasons and led the team in receiving in eight of those seasons. He was also part of a powerful Eagles team that included running back Steve Van Buren and quarterback Tommy Thompson.

That first season Neale devised the Pihos Screen, a pass thrown behind the line of scrimmage to the tight end, which stretched rival defenses to the limit.

In his first three seasons, the Eagles were 28–7–1 and went to the NFL Championship Game each year, winning the last two. And while the team's fortunes leveled out in the next few years, Pihos continued to be the star.

In 1952, with the defection of Bud Grant to the Canadian Football League, the Eagles needed a defensive end. They called on Pihos to play the position along with his duties on offense, and he was named All-Pro at defensive end too.

Following the 1955 season, at only 32 years old, Pihos decided to retire. He knew he could still play, but Trimble was gone, and he could see the Eagles were headed for a fall. He also recalled a meeting he'd had with Joe DiMaggio, the New York Yankees star. DiMaggio told Pihos that when he decided to retire, he should go out on top. "Don't go out as a has-been," DiMaggio said.

"I always remembered that," Pihos said. "I could've played longer, but I decided to retire on top."

No one will dispute that he did, and in 1970, the Golden Greek was inducted into the Pro Football Hall of Fame.

In 2001, Pihos was diagnosed with Alzheimer's disease, and died in 2011 in North Carolina. His daughter, Melissa, would go on to produce a series of documentaries about her dad and his struggles with the disease that, she hopes, will help other families.

28 Wilbert Montgomery

For a four-year period from 1978 through 1981, there was no better running back in the NFC than Wilbert Montgomery.

He was one of those backs—the way Detroit's Barry Sanders and Minnesota's Adrian Peterson were later on—who caused rival defenses to tense up every time he touched the ball. He could score from anywhere on the field and could make yardage when it seemed none was available. "When Wilbert is healthy, he is the finest player in the game," Eagles quarterback Ron Jaworski said during Montgomery's prime years.

In his eight seasons with the Eagles, he set seven Eagles rushing records, including career attempts (1,465), rushing yards (6,538), season rushes (338 in 1979), rushing yards in a season (1,512 in 1979), career 100-yard games (26), 100-yard rushing games in a season (8 in 1981), and touchdowns in a game (4). Not bad for a guy few considered much of a pro prospect when he was taken in the sixth round of the 1977 draft, an undersized back drafted out of the small Abilene Christian.

He showed up to the Eagles as a painfully shy player lacking the kind of confidence normally attributed to young players who think they can do anything. Montgomery was so reticent with the media that he would spend hours in the training room so he wouldn't have to speak to anyone. Jaworski said Montgomery even stuffed a towel under his door during training camp so coaches couldn't slide a pink slip (meaning he'd been cut) under his door.

"He didn't think he'd make the team," Jaworski said. "But everyone else in camp recognized his talent. He had everything it takes to make it in the NFL. The only thing he lacked was confidence."

But he had plenty of that when he stepped on the field, and he showed it in his second season in 1978 when he rushed for 1,220 yards, Philly's first 1,000-yard rushing performance since Steve Van Buren in 1949.

The next season, he put together the best season an Eagle has ever had, rolling to a club-record 1,512 yards on a team-record 338 carries. It was a season for the ages, and the Eagles thrived, posting an 11–5 record. But after winning their first playoff game for the first time since 1960, the Eagles were stunned by the Tampa Bay Buccaneers in the second round, and Montgomery's Herculean effort was for naught.

Ironically, it was in 1980, a season in which Montgomery was plagued by injuries, that the Eagles finally got over the hump. Montgomery played only 12 regular-season games and was held to 778 rushing yards. But by the time the playoffs rolled around, Montgomery was healthy again, and that's what made the difference in the Eagles' title run.

Philly hosted the NFC Championship Game against the hated Cowboys, and Montgomery was battling a strained knee and a bruised hip but, as he said afterward, "You come this far, you don't sit down for a little pain."

On the game's second play, Montgomery took a handoff from Jaworski, broke through a huge hole, and ran 42 yards for the critical first score of the game.

Against a Cowboys defense that hadn't allowed a 100-yard performance in 29 straight postseason games, Montgomery carved up Dallas for 194 yards on 26 carries, and the Eagles handily won 20–7 and earned a spot in their first Super Bowl.

In many ways, it was Montgomery's crowning moment for the Eagles, though he did set the team rushing record in 1984. But by that stage, injuries had really begun to take their toll. After that season, he was traded to the Detroit Lions for linebacker Garry Cobb. He played just seven games for the Lions and retired.

Montgomery has stayed in the NFL. In 1997 he was hired by his former coach, Dick Vermeil, to coach running backs in St. Louis. He later went to the Baltimore Ravens and was the Ravens' running-backs coach through the 2013 season. He then joined the Cleveland Browns as running-backs coach in 2014 but was fired after the 2015 season along with head coach Mike Pettine and the rest of his staff.

29 The Fog Bowl

Perhaps the most amazing part of the game that would come to be known as the "the Fog Bowl" was that the day began sunny and clear with temperatures in the upper 30s—paradise in Chicago in midwinter.

But while the day may have started that way, it did not finish that way and, because it didn't, the game that ensued has found its way into pro football lore and legend.

The bullet point for the NFC Divisional Playoff on December 31, 1988, should have been the return to Chicago of former Bears defensive coordinator Buddy Ryan, who was now head coach of the Eagles.

It started like a thousand other games. The Bears controlled the game early, and when Kevin Butler kicked a field goal to extend Chicago's lead to 17–6, nothing seemed out of the ordinary.

Then the fog began to roll in. Not a light, feathery fog, either. It was thick and heavy and gray and ominous, like something more suited to a Scottish moor. And it didn't come slowly either. It landed with a thud. One minute it wasn't there, and 10 minutes later, no one could see anything. Eagles defensive end Reggie White thought it was smoke from a nearby fire, as did Bears quarterback Mike Tomczak, who said, "I thought the parking lot was on fire."

"It was crazy," said Mike Ditka. "All we needed was Count Dracula at quarterback."

The fog proved so thick and pervasive that fans could not see what was transpiring on the field. TV and radio announcers had no idea what was happening, and the public-address announcer simply gave up trying to explain what he couldn't see.

So what happened? Meteorologically speaking, warming air on land mixed with the dense colder air over Lake Michigan, and the result was epic fog.

When the fog got serious in the third quarter, referee Jim Tunney, who had control once the game began, asked both coaches if they wanted to continue, and each said yes. Tunney said he was told by the NFL to continue the game no matter what, despite some complaints from players. "It looked worse from the stands because they had the lights on, and it reflected off the fog," he said. "On the field, the fog was patchy. There were pockets that were clear, others that were thick."

Most players disputed that. "I couldn't see the other end of the field," Eagles quarterback Randall Cunningham said.

And in the second half, anything resembling offense ground to a halt. "We could probably have had the whole team out on the field and no one would have known it," Cunningham said. "Maybe that's what we should have done."

It was too bad the fog impacted the game the way it did, because the game featured two of the NFL's most entertaining teams with head coaches—once friends—who were now bitter rivals.

And as much as Cunningham complained about the conditions, he threw for 407 yards, with tight end Keith Jackson catching seven passes for 142 yards. But he also dropped a touchdown pass and two other Eagles touchdowns were wiped out by penalties.

In the end, the Bears won the game 20–12 and, to this day, the Eagles swear the result would have been different in better weather. "Half the game was played in sunshine, and they couldn't get the ball in the end zone," Ditka said later. "If they can't score in the sunlight, it's not our fault."

30 The 1980 Eagles

There remains something about the 1980 Eagles that is vaguely lovable, sort of admirable, and downright impressive.

This was not a great football team, and even the guys who played for it would probably admit that. They had some good talent, not great. They had players who had put together good seasons, not spectacular seasons. But when it came time to get the job done, they could always be counted on. "We had a lot of confidence as a team," said quarterback Ron Jaworski.

Indeed, no one had more confidence than he did, and whatever the 1980 Eagles were, it was largely due to what he provided. "We felt whatever we needed to do to win, we could do it," he said. "The offense was solid, the defense was consistent, and we had good special teams. It was just a great bunch of guys who understood their roles, loved to play, and loved being Eagles."

Maybe that's why that bunch continues to hold such a fond place in the hearts of most Eagles fans. Yes, that was the team that ended a long drought and brought the city its first league title in 20 years as well as its first Super Bowl berth. And while the Super Bowl then was not the national extravaganza it is today, it was building momentum in that direction, and getting there most certainly mattered.

Even if that bunch hadn't accomplished what it did, there was still something special, in a ragged way, about those Eagles.

In some ways, a spot in Super Bowl XV was the next logical step for this team. This was, after all, year No. 5 in the five-year plan of coach Dick Vermeil. He had come to the Eagles from UCLA, young and enthusiastic and brimming with confidence, but he was also smart enough to know nothing was going to happen overnight. The first two years were to get the plan in place. The next two would be to get the personnel in the right place. The fifth, in Vermeil's mind, was when it should all come together.

But this was not one of these teams of the ages, full of incredible talent at every position. It was a team of players who knew their roles well, did not complain (well, not a lot), and performed to the best of their ability for the good of the team. "We work hard because that's what I believe in," Vermeil said at the time. "We're preparing players for 11 individual wars every Sunday. I'm tough on them because I feel it's necessary."

Players often talked of the tough, long practices during which the only input from coaches was usually negative. But every player suffered through it, and players drew closer together because they were all in the same boat.

Veteran linebacker Bill Bergey, whose last game was the Super Bowl, saw what Vermeil was doing. "He was getting rid of the whiners and losers and finding guys who were tough enough to play his brand of football," he said.

And it all fell together magnificently that season. The Eagles overcame injuries to the likes of leading rusher Wilbert Montgomery, leading receiver Harold Carmichael, and even Jaworski. But they had guys who could fill in superbly, like little running back Louis Giammona—who also happened to be Vermeil's nephew—and quarterback Joe Pisarcik.

The Eagles ran off 11 wins in their first 12 games but then hit a roadblock that tested Vermeil's theory about how tough a unit he really had. They lost by a point in San Diego and by three points to the Atlanta Falcons before beating the St. Louis Cardinals.

Then came the season finale in Texas Stadium against the Cowboys, who had been breathing down Philly's neck all season. In a weird twist, the Cowboys, who were 11–4, could only win the NFC East if they beat the Eagles by 25 points or more.

Since the league-leading Eagles defense hadn't surrendered more than 24 points all season, no one seemed too concerned until the Cowboys jumped out to a 21–0 lead and led 35–10 in the fourth quarter. Jaworski recalls looking at the scoreboard in disbelief. *This can't be happening,* he thought. *We can't blow this.*

The Eagles did score three times but still lost 35–27, giving them three losses in their last four games heading into the playoffs.

The malaise continued in the first half of Philly's playoff opener against the Minnesota Vikings when the heavily favored Eagles were behind 14–0 in the second quarter. Despite a spate of injuries on both sides of the ball, Vermeil had no sympathy for his battered team. Neither did Eagles defensive coordinator Marion Campbell, who lit into his troops at halftime. After telling them everything they had done wrong in the first 30 minutes, he ended with this: "You're a great defense. Now play like one."

The Eagles defense responded by forcing eight second-half turnovers, including five interceptions, and sacking Vikings quarterback Tommy Kramer three times. The Eagles also mustered enough offense to win 31–16, setting up the NFC Championship Game at Veterans Stadium against—who else?—the Dallas Cowboys.

The teams had split their regular-season games, but in a brilliant piece of gamesmanship, as the home team, the Eagles had the choice of what color jerseys to wear. For years, the Eagles had worn green jerseys at home, but this time, Vermeil had a plan.

He knew how much the Cowboys hated wearing their blue jerseys, and they rarely did because, in truth, many in the organization thought it was bad luck. So instead of wearing their traditional home green, Vermeil chose their usual white road jerseys, forcing the Cowboys to wear the blue they despised. Reportedly Cowboys team president Tex Schramm was furious when he learned what the Eagles had done. "It was just one more thing for them to think about," Vermeil said.

On the field, it was more of the same. Despite a series of injuries, Montgomery played like a man possessed. He scored, untouched, on a 42-yard run on the game's second play, and the Eagles defense never gave the Cowboys a chance to breathe. They

The Vatican's Team

Those 1980 Eagles also had one other thing going for them: Pope John Paul II. Sometimes, a little extra help never hurts.

It's not known if the Pope actually found a TV in the Vatican and watched the Eagles play the Raiders on that January evening in 1981, but it would be an interesting situation to imagine.

Here are the details of how the Eagles became the Vatican's team—sort of.

A year earlier, when John Paul was visiting Philadelphia, Eagles general manager Jim Murray, whose infant son was also named John Paul, caught the pontiff's eye in a crowd after he saw the youngster carrying a sign that read, "I, too, am called John Paul, named in your honor for His glory."

The pope met with the child, and the Eagles' photographer, Ed Mahan, happened to catch the perfect photo of pontiff and child, and the photo was shown everywhere.

In December 1980 Ed Piszek, a Philadelphia businessman and a longtime friend of the Pope from their days in Poland as well as of Eagles owner Leonard Tose and Murray, was visiting John Paul in Rome and brought the photo.

The pope recalled the incident and asked who Jim Murray was and what he did. Told he was involved with a pro football team that was playing for a championship, the pontiff grew even more interested.

He also smiled when told the Eagles had two Polish quarterbacks—Ron Jaworski and Joe Pisarcik. "I wouldn't want them to get hurt," he said, so he produced two papal medals, blessed them, and told Piszek to give them to the players, which he did at a team meeting later that week.

"Our two quarterbacks have got to feel pretty good," Murray said that day. "Now they've got [offensive linemen] Stan Walters, Jerry Sisemore, and the pope protecting them. That's three Pro Bowlers right there."

forced four turnovers, Montgomery ran for 194 yards, and the Eagles won 20–7, securing their first trip to the Super Bowl.

"The final score was not indicative of how dominant we were," Bergey said later. "We could've played 20 more quarters, and the Cowboys would not have scored another touchdown." The city erupted in joy. The years of agony were over, and the Eagles, so long maligned and so often just an afterthought, were playing in the NFL's premier game.

Jaworski threw for 3,529 yards and 27 touchdowns and was named the NFC's Player of the Year. Montgomery was the team's top rusher with 778 yards, but Leroy Harris and Giammona also contributed mightily. The defense forced 25 interceptions with Brenard Wilson (six) and Roynell Young (four) leading the way.

The Eagles had finally reached one of their ultimate goals. All that stood in the way of completing the task were the Oakland Raiders in Super Bowl XV.

31 Michael Vick

He has been to hell and back, and somehow Michael Vick has survived.

True, the hell was of Vick's making, and whatever he has suffered through—and it has been plenty—he needs only to look in the mirror to find the reason why it happened. But the fact remains that his is a story of redemption, rebirth, and taking advantage of a second chance few thought he would ever receive.

His sincerity has been, and will continue to be, questioned by a large segment of society and sports fans, horrified by what he was convicted of. But the fact remains that when given an opportunity to try again, he succeeded spectacularly.

The Eagles will forever be known as the team that either gave a convicted felon (who had served his time) the second chance everyone deserves or the team that enabled a cruel, thoughtless superstar who thought he was above the law.

Few people fall anywhere in the middle when it comes to the former Virginia Tech and Atlanta Falcons star. But when Vick signed with the Eagles in August 2009, after more than two years away from football, few thought it was anything more than a fool's errand. Make no mistake, the Eagles received a torrent of criticism from animal-rights groups horrified that any team would bring him back, especially considering his crime.

In 2007 Vick, who was then near the top of the NFL pyramid with the Falcons, was implicated in a dog-fighting ring that he had allegedly operated for more than five years. Stories became public of Vick's torture of dogs and how, when pressed on the details of the Bad Newz Kennels he owned, he denied any knowledge of mistreatment.

But soon the mountain of evidence piled up and, in August 2007, Vick pleaded guilty to federal charges and was sentenced to 21 months in federal prison. But that was only the beginning.

The wrath of the NFL came next, and commissioner Roger Goodell suspended Vick indefinitely. Later that month, the Falcons cut ties with their once-prized quarterback, also demanding a return of the $20 million signing bonus he received.

Meanwhile, Vick served his sentence and was all but forgotten by the NFL. After all, it's hard enough to play in the NFL without taking a break. Imagine a player trying to come back after two years away.

But Vick was released from prison in July 2009 and immediately set about the task of rebuilding his life and his career. Once cleared by Goodell, Vick received several offers but ended

Eagles backup quarterback Michael Vick sits on the bench before replacing starting quarterback Donovan McNabb for the final possession of a 40–17 Eagles win over the New York Giants on November 1, 2009.

up signing a two-year deal with the Eagles. The signing caused a firestorm, and the Eagles spent weeks defending it. "I'm a believer that as long as people go through the right process, they deserve a second chance," Eagles coach Andy Reid said.

General manager Joe Banner took his share of heat too but tried to explain that the Eagles were not going out on a limb with the signing. "It was very tough initially, but everybody we talked to said the same thing," Banner said. "He was remorseful and he had gone through an incredible transformation. I just hope people understand that we did our research."

But a lot of people didn't understand that, and they were furious with the franchise. Many fans boycotted games, and some gave up their season tickets.

But Vick did all the right things and said all the right things and watched dutifully as the No. 3 quarterback behind Donovan McNabb and Kevin Kolb. He played in 12 games that first season and tried to stay out of the limelight.

By 2010, though, much had changed. McNabb, who had lobbied the Eagles hard to sign Vick, had been traded and Kolb was installed as the new starter with Vick as his backup. And that seemed to be that. But in the season opener against Green Bay, Kolb suffered a concussion, and Vick stepped in and set the NFL on its ear.

Unprepared for Vick's scrambling, the Packers chased him all over the Linc, and Vick responded superbly. He completed 16 of 24 passes for 175 yards and a touchdown and ran for another 103 yards in barely three quarters of work that nearly brought the Eagles to a come-from-behind win.

Just a few days later, Reid declared Vick would be the starter for the rest of the season. In his first NFL start in three years, Vick threw for 284 yards and two touchdowns against the Detroit Lions and followed it up with a 291-yard performance against the Jacksonville Jaguars. And though he was hurt the next week against

Washington and missed the next three games, he was still named the NFC Offensive Player of the Month.

When Vick returned from his injury, he retook his starting job from Kolb and was better than before. In the end, he helped guide the Eagles to a 10–6 record and an NFC East title. He threw for 3,018 yards, 21 touchdowns, and was intercepted just six times in 12 games and ran for another 676 yards and nine more touchdowns. He earned his fourth Pro Bowl selection and was named the league's Comeback Player of the Year.

That's not to say he accomplished this in a vacuum. There are dozens of websites that still attack Vick and claim he is not sincere about changing. And Vick did not help himself late in the season when he suggested to an interviewer that one day he'd like to own dogs again.

He is also not earning the money from the contract he signed, as much of it is going to legal fees and to bookkeepers trying to settle his bankruptcy.

In February 2011 Vick was named the Eagles' franchise player and was all but handed the starting quarterback job for the foreseeable future. He also signed a one-year tender worth $20 million.

Vick would perform well that season and played for the Eagles through 2013. In 2014, he signed with the New York Jets but injury cut his season short. In 2015, he signed with the Pittsburgh Steelers but after that season he saw the writing on the wall and officially retired with the team that drafted him, the Atlanta Falcons.

Vick is now trying his hand at coaching after his old Eagles' coach, Andy Reid, hired him as a summer coaching intern with the Chiefs in 2017.

Pete Retzlaff

Not a bad deal for $100. That's what the Philadelphia Eagles paid to claim one Pete Retzlaff off waivers after the Detroit Lions had cut him in 1956. In return, all Retzlaff provided was 11 quality years of service in which he took his place as one of the best receivers in football, assumed the reins as Eagles general manager for four years and, even now, remains one of the most respected and liked players in organization history.

His 452 career receptions remain second in team history, as are his 7,412 receiving yards. His 204 yards in a single game (November 14, 1965, against the Redskins) is third all-time. He also remains in the franchise's top five in touchdown receptions with 47.

And this was a guy no one really knew what to do with when he came out of South Dakota State in 1953. He was drafted by the Detroit Lions in the 22nd round (at a time when there were 30 rounds in the draft), but they weren't sure where to put him. Eventually they tried him at fullback but ultimately cut him. He went into the army for the next two years and, in 1956, Eagles general manager Vince McNally decided to take a chance on him since they really had nothing to lose (the Eagles were 4–7–1 the year before). "And the Eagles had no idea what to do with me either," Retzlaff recalled.

He was tried at running back in his first training camp and was the leading rusher in the preseason before he was moved to wide receiver. But in his first two seasons, Retzlaff left an impression on no one, catching just 22 passes.

In 1958, though, everything changed. Well, one specific thing changed, and that was the Eagles' acquisition of veteran quarterback

Norm Van Brocklin from the Los Angeles Rams. "The best thing that ever happened to me was the trade for Norm Van Brocklin," Retzlaff said. "The first year he was in camp, he was watching the receivers, and he said, 'You know, that Retzlaff runs patterns a lot like [eventual Hall of Famer] Elroy Hirsch.'"

Such a compliment from a player of Van Brocklin's stature did wonders for Retzlaff's confidence, and he responded with the first of what would be a series of terrific, consistent seasons.

In 1958, playing on a horrid Eagles team, Retzlaff caught 56 passes, tying him for the league lead with Baltimore's Raymond Berry.

By 1960 the Eagles found themselves among the league's top teams, and Retzlaff teamed up with fellow wide receiver Tommy McDonald to provide a lethal combination. Retzlaff was the team's leading receiver with 46 receptions, while McDonald was the game-breaker, catching 39 passes, with 13 going for touchdowns. With those two catching passes and Van Brocklin flinging them, the Eagles beat the Packers to win their first NFL title in 11 years.

Between 1958 and 1962, Retzlaff and McDonald formed an incomparable receiving duo. McDonald caught 237 passes in that period (third-best among all receivers), and Retzlaff wasn't far behind, catching another 216 passes (No. 5 on that list).

McDonald was eventually traded and, in 1963, Retzlaff became the Eagles' go-to guy and would be the team's leading receiver for the next four seasons. And in 1964 he made a major change, shifting from split end to tight end. In 1965 he set career bests in receptions (66), yards (1,190), and touchdowns (10). For that performance, he was named NFL Player of the Year by several organizations. "That was arguably the best season a tight end ever had," said Berry, another good tight end, who even made a film reel of Retzlaff's season in order to study his moves.

In 1966 Retzlaff caught another 40 passes and decided it was time to retire after 11 seasons and five trips to the Pro Bowl.

He spent the next two years doing radio and TV work when, in 1969, new Eagles owner Leonard Tose hired Retzlaff to become general manager, replacing the virulently unpopular coach/GM Joe Kuharich.

But Retzlaff's popularity as a player did not translate to his new role in the front office. He hired Jerry Williams as head coach (he would last barely two seasons), and in his first draft, he selected Purdue running back Leroy Keyes, who held out in a contract dispute until September.

It only got worse after that. Over the next four seasons, the Eagles won just 15 games, and in December 1972 Retzlaff resigned to run his business interests in Texas and in his home state of South Dakota.

"I can judge talent," Retzlaff said later of his difficult years as the Eagles GM. "But it's difficult to put the right team on the field with the right attitude. We inherited some guys who weren't interested in dedicating themselves to winning football games. I tried it [being general manager], and I was glad to leave."

Retzlaff remains an icon among Eagles fans and still attends games frequently. He was named to the Eagles Honor Roll and had his No. 44 retired.

And all that for $100.

33 DeSean Jackson

It may go too far to say DeSean Jackson is the most exciting player in Philadelphia Eagles history. But you'd be hard-pressed to find someone who tops him.

Jackson is the proverbial player who can seemingly score from anywhere because…well…he has proven he can. Whether a wide receiver, runner, or kick returner, Jackson has become one of those players in the NFL who causes opposing defensive coordinators to hold their breath when he touches the ball.

Through the 2010 season, the University of California product, drafted in the second round of the 2008 draft, has already been named to two Pro Bowls, and with his four punt returns for touchdowns, he is already the team's all-time leader.

He's one of only two players in NFL history (Washington's Dick Todd was the other in 1941) to score touchdowns via reception, rushing, and punt returns in each of their first three seasons. Since 2008 he also leads the NFL by averaging 18.2 yards per catch and has 1,112 punt-return yards. In 2009 he was the only player in NFL history to be named to the Pro Bowl at two different positions—wide receiver and punt returner. And, oh yes, he's already caught 171 passes in just three seasons. Of his 26 touchdowns, 19 have come from at least 30 yards. In fact, since entering the league, 14 of his touchdowns have come from at least 50 yards out, another NFL record.

In one especially memorable sequence in 2010, Jackson scored on an 88-yard toss from Michael Vick and then, less than a month later, scored from 91 yards out against Dallas.

Of course, what most Eagles fans know Jackson for is his incredible punt return against the New York Giants in 2010 on

Wide receiver DeSean Jackson poses with a football after learning that he has been selected by the Philadelphia Eagles in the second round of the NFL Draft on April 26, 2008.

the game's last play. Dubbed "the Miracle at the Meadowlands II," Jackson fielded the kick in the game's waning seconds, broke up the middle, and scored as time expired, diving into the end zone for the touchdown. The loss all but ended the Giants' playoffs hopes and helped propel the Eagles to the top of the NFC East. "Most incredible thing I've ever seen," coach Andy Reid said.

There were questions about Jackson's durability because of his size—5'10", 170 pounds—but through his first three seasons, he missed just three games.

But it hasn't all been smooth sailing between Jackson and the Eagles. After his first two remarkable seasons, he wanted to renegotiate his contract, and the Eagles refused. He skipped the team's voluntary (though highly recommended) off-season camp, enraging Reid. He also refused to speak with the media as part of his protest. But in the end, he reported. And despite missing two games (one with a serious concussion), he still caught 47 passes and averaged more than 22 yards per catch in 2010.

His battles in Philly continued in 2011, when he did not report to training camp in July, though he did show up a week later and played well. In 2012, the Eagles placed the franchise tag on Jackson to keep him on the team and a few weeks later inked him to a new five-year, $51 millions deal. He continued his strong play and battled through injury and controversy to stake his place as one of the Eagles' top receiving threats.

But after the 2013 season, he was released and signed by the Washington Redskins, where he remained for three seasons before signing with the Tampa Bay Buccaneers in 2017.

And though he's been gone for several seasons, Jackson is still fourth all-time in team history with 6,117 receiving yards and eighth all-time in receptions with 356.

34 Al Wistert

For the Eagles of the mid-1940s to the early 1950s, the name that stood out, of course, was Steve Van Buren. He was the team's top player, the leading rusher, and the guy who helped lead the Eagles to three straight trips to the NFL Championship Game and two championships.

But look a little closer, and there was more to that team than just the running of Van Buren. "Al was the glue that kept that team together," quarterback Bill Mackrides said.

"Al" was Al Wistert, an exceptional offensive and defensive lineman who was named All-Pro in eight of his nine seasons with the Eagles. He was the guy generally credited with opening the holes Van Buren ran through, and his contemporaries routinely called him the finest lineman of the era.

He joined the Eagles in 1943 after a stellar college career at the University of Michigan. The Eagles thought so highly of him, they signed him for what was then the staggering sum of $4,500. A number of players initially resented him for his salary, but when they saw his determination and ability, they decided maybe he was worth it. And he became a teammate everyone could rely on.

The late head coach George Allen, in his book *Pro Football's 100 Greatest Players*, listed Wistert as one of the 10 greatest defensive linemen in NFL history. But he's also the only one of those 10 who is not in the Pro Football Hall of Fame. And therein lies the story.

It is generally considered that, at least through 2010, the two players who should be in the hallowed halls of Canton, Ohio, but are not are Green Bay Packers guard Jerry Kramer and, more recently, Minnesota Vikings wide receiver Cris Carter. There has always been a small but vocal group who believe Wistert deserves the same consideration.

His consistency and years as an All-Pro, and the fact that he played both offense and defense for an Eagles team that was one of the best in the league at the time, seem to be more than enough to get Wistert in. But to date, nothing has happened, despite the fact that his coach, Greasy Neale, and four teammates—Chuck Bednarik, Pete Pihos, Alex Wojciechowicz, and Van Buren—are in.

One of the toughest players of the era, Wistert recounted a story from a game in the mid-1940s when he came to the sideline limping.

"I think I broke my leg," Wistert told coach Greasy Neale.

"You think you did?" Neale asked. "Well, go back in there and run around and make sure."

He did.

Wistert, as with many players of the era, retired relatively early, after just nine seasons. He quit in 1951 because, at age 31, he felt his skills were diminishing and he didn't want to stay around and confirm his suspicion.

"Pro football is a great game as long as you're able to give more than you receive," he told the Associated Press at the time. "In the past few years, I've reached the point where the receiving is getting the edge."

He left the game on his terms and retired to the West Coast, where he became an insurance agent. And, from afar, he watched as others continued their campaign to get him Hall of Fame recognition.

He may not be there yet, but he was named to the NFL's All-Decade Team of the 1940s, was inducted into the Eagles Honor Roll in 2009, and saw his No. 70 retired by the team, the first uniform ever retired by the franchise.

In 1963, though, that number was mistakenly reissued to Jim Skaggs, who was allowed to wear it until his retirement in 1972, when it was retired again—this time permanently.

35 Brian Westbrook

It was one of the hardest conversations Andy Reid ever had to conduct. After the 2009 season, the Eagles head coach could see the handwriting on the wall as it pertained to one of his favorite players of all time. Injuries had slowed him down, and the development of a younger player had pushed Reid to a decision he had hoped never to have to make—he was going to have to tell running back Brian Westbrook his days as an Eagle were over.

"I think we all know that Brian Westbrook is one of the all-time great Philadelphia Eagles," Reid said after delivering the news to the eight-year veteran. "For what we've done here over the years, Brian has been a huge part of building this program to the level that we're at now. My heart will always be a Brian Westbrook fan as we go forward here."

A two-time All-Pro who, in 2007, had the kind of season that defines "all-around athlete," Westbrook departed as the team's second all-time leading rusher with 5,995 yards, second only to Wilbert Montgomery. His 426 receptions, whether it was from the backfield or as a slot receiver, is third-best in team history, and his 68 total touchdowns—from rushing, receiving, and returns—is third-best.

And perhaps the most incredible part is that, due to a seemingly never-ending spate of injuries, Westbrook never played a full 16-game season.

"He had no weaknesses," Reid said. "There wasn't any one thing you could pick out that he wasn't good at."

The Eagles thought they had a good idea of what they were getting when they made him their third-round draft pick in 2002. He would be a good third-down back catching the ball out of the backfield, he could return kicks and, if he could stay healthy (he missed his entire sophomore season at Villanova due to a knee injury), he might pick up some yardage as a running back. "He's a very exciting player," Reid said at the time. He had no idea.

The Eagles understood quickly just how special he was and used him brilliantly. In fact, he was every bit as dangerous as a receiver as he was a running back, and often defenses simply didn't know how to adjust to Westbrook and what he provided.

In his second season, he teamed up with fellow running backs Duce Staley and Correll Buckhalter to form the "Three-Headed Monster" backfield, and Westbrook was the leading rusher with 613 yards and 13 touchdowns.

Staley left for free agency the following season, and Buckhalter suffered a season-ending knee injury in the preseason. The load fell exclusively on Westbrook, who responded with more than 1,500 yards from scrimmage—and he didn't play the last two games because Reid wanted to rest him.

If they didn't know it before, the Eagles had figured out by then just what a versatile weapon Westbrook was.

In 2006 he was everywhere—at running back and wide receiver and a slot receiver—and his 1,916 yards from scrimmage were more than 31 percent of the Eagles' total offense.

In 2007 he was even more dominant. Playing in 15 games, he rushed for 1,333 yards (the fourth-best performance in team history) and caught 90 passes (still a team record) for another 771 yards, for 2,104 total yards. That was an astonishing 37 percent of the team's total offense.

Despite playing just 14 games in 2008, he still accounted for 1,338 total yards (24 percent of the offense), but it was clear the injuries to his knees and triceps over the years were starting to take their toll.

In 2009 he missed half the season with two different concussions and an ankle injury and, by that point, a rookie from Pittsburgh named LeSean McCoy seemed ready to take over. So in February 2010 Reid informed Westbrook he was being released to make room for the inevitable next generation. "Tough day," Reid said.

Westbrook did sign with the San Francisco 49ers and played well, but as of the end of the 2010 season, he was again looking for a place to play. He said in March 2011 that he wanted to return to the Eagles to conclude his career, but the Eagles had not responded.

Nonetheless, according to Reid, "He is a Philadelphia Eagle."

36 Ollie Matson

Sometimes it's not about years of service, yardage gained, or the number of catches or quarterback sacks. Sometimes it's about getting one more chance to prove yourself. And sometimes that's what is most important.

Consider the case of running back Ollie Matson, who played the final three seasons of his stellar NFL career in Philadelphia. Matson owed nothing to the game. He was an All-American at the University of San Francisco and a six-time Pro Bowler in his first seven seasons with the Chicago Cardinals. He was one of the great athletes of the 1950s, a two-time Olympic medalist in the 1952 Summer Games and the Cardinals' first-round draft pick that same year. He was the guy everyone meant when they said he could score from anywhere on the field. And he could. Big, strong, and fast, he had everything. And when he was through, he had piled up 12,799 all-purpose yards, the second-best in NFL history behind the inimitable Jim Brown.

But by 1959 it was obvious the Cardinals weren't going anywhere, so they dealt him to the Los Angeles Rams, who essentially traded the bulk of their team to get him. He spent four seasons with the Rams and one miserable season in 1963 with the Detroit Lions, during which he rarely got off the bench.

That's when he got one more chance. Joe Kuharich, the Eagles' coach at the time, had coached Matson in college and had always called him the best athlete he had ever seen. In 1964 he brought Matson to the Eagles, not to set more league records but to provide his old pupil a chance to go out on his terms.

It was a move Matson never forgot. "Everyone had written me off," Matson said years later. "They thought I was too old, but Joe still believed in me. He gave me a chance, and I proved I could still play."

Indeed, Matson split time at halfback with Timmy Brown and also returned punts and kicks. When Brown got hurt late that season, Matson went in at running back and scored two key touchdowns late in an Eagles win.

After the 1966 season, Matson retired, satisfied he had proved his point. Matson often called his three seasons in Philly the most satisfying of his career.

Matson was inducted into the Pro Football Hall of Fame in 1972 and acknowledged the Eagles at the time.

In February 2011 he died of respiratory failure at age 80.

37 Eric Allen

There was no pressure on Eric Allen when he joined the Philadelphia Eagles in 1988. No, no pressure at all. All the team did was trade up nine spots in the second round of the draft so coach Buddy Ryan, who had specifically targeted the Arizona State product, could take him. And all he was expected to do was anchor an inexperienced secondary and help become the defensive force that Ryan expected. Looking back, Allen did all that and more in his seven years with the Eagles.

Indeed, he became the backbone of one of the most fearsome defenses the NFL has seen. In its heyday, the defense consisted of the likes of Reggie White, Jerome Brown, Clyde Simmons, Seth Joyner, and William Thomas. That defense was nicknamed "Gang Green," and the players loved it.

And in the middle of all of that was Allen. He was a five-time Pro Bowler and remains tied for the team record (with Bill Bradley and Brian Dawkins) with 34 career interceptions and holds the team record for most interceptions returned for a touchdown (five). He was fast and smart and often knew what the quarterback was going to do with the ball before the quarterback did.

In 1989 Allen was part of a defense that set a club record with 62 quarterback sacks and forced an NFL-best 56 takeaways, including 30 interceptions. Eight of those picks went to Allen.

He never had fewer than three interceptions in any season with the Eagles and, in 1993, he picked off six passes and returned four of them for touchdowns, still an NFC record.

"He was my favorite defensive back of all time," Ryan said later. "When I first saw him on film, he just stood out. He plays the game all the way to the hilt."

Allen signed a free-agent deal with the New Orleans Saints after the 1994 season, part of the mass exodus of Eagles players who couldn't get the money they thought they deserved in Philadelphia.

He played three seasons with the Saints, where he earned one more Pro Bowl berth, then he played four seasons in Oakland before retiring.

Allen, who now works as an analyst with ESPN, was also named to the Eagles 75th Anniversary Team.

38 Jim Johnson

Jim Johnson always scoffed at any suggestion he was some kind of defensive "genius." All he did, he said time and time again, was put players in the right position, and they did the rest. But it was not the simple.

For 10 seasons, the Philadelphia Eagles put one of the most aggressive, dominating, entertaining, confusing defenses on the field, and it all sprouted from the fertile mind and, yes, *genius* of defensive coordinator Jim Johnson.

But it wouldn't have been possible if Andy Reid—young, untested, and with no head-coaching experience—hadn't targeted the veteran Johnson in 1999 to be his defensive coordinator. And once he did, the Eagles almost immediately became one of the NFL's best defenses. The architect was Johnson, whose philosophy was to always make an offense uncomfortable. To do that, Johnson came up with blitz packages that defied belief. He would sometimes draw up new ones the day of a game and present them to his defense, which would howl in delight at the sheer audacity of it all.

What made Johnson's job even easier was the fact that Reid, an offensive guru, decided early on that the defense would belong to Johnson, and Johnson alone. That confidence allowed him to do the kinds of things other defensive coordinators might not try. "Jim Johnson is the best in the business at what he does," Reid said in 2005 when Johnson was given a contract extension that made him the highest-paid coordinator in the league.

The numbers bore that out. From 2000 to 2007, the Eagles defense posted 342 quarterback sacks, the most in the league. In 2001 Johnson's unit became just the fourth in NFL history to hold all 16 opponents to 21 points or fewer. And that streak eventually extended to 34 straight games, the second-best in league history. In 1999 the Eagles defense forced an NFL-best 46 turnovers, including a team-record five interceptions that were returned for touchdowns. Eagles defenders also racked up 26 Pro Bowl nods.

More to the point, the Eagles won. From 1999 to 2009 there were five NFC East titles, eight playoff appearances, five trips to the NFC Championship Game, and one Super Bowl.

As good as Johnson was, there really wasn't much in his coaching history to suggest he'd be the defensive stalwart he ended up being. His coaching career began at Missouri Southern College in 1967, and his journey took him to other college programs like Drake, Indiana, and Notre Dame, where he was promoted to defensive coordinator in 1982.

He left the college ranks in 1984, spending two seasons in the ill-fated USFL before joining the Cardinals in 1986, first as defensive line coach and then as a secondary coach. He then went on to the Indianapolis Colts and spent one season as linebackers coach with the Seattle Seahawks before he came to Philly to stay.

In January 2009 it was announced that Johnson would take a leave of absence after a tumor on his spine was discovered. In his stead, secondary coach and Johnson disciple Sean McDermott took over as interim defensive coordinator. On July 24, 2009, Johnson officially resigned as defensive coordinator and, just four days later, he was dead at age 68.

One of his former players, safety Brian Dawkins, mourned his passing. "He was a tough coach who wasn't afraid to let you know what he was feeling. But at the same time, he cared deeply about us."

McDermott said the only way he knew how to coach defense was by what Johnson had taught him. "What hasn't he taught me?" McDermott said. But the same success did not extend to

Johnson's understudy. After two seasons as defensive coordinator, McDermott was fired by Reid.

Perhaps it was just another example of how, in more ways than one, Jim Johnson was irreplaceable.

39 Fourth-and-26

Those three words say it all. Nothing else needs to be added, nothing else explained, nothing else clarified. To Eagles fans, it remains one of the great plays in team history—perhaps the greatest, considering the circumstances—while to Green Bay Packers loyalists it will always be a reason to drive one's head through a wall.

It happened on January 11, 2004, as the Eagles hosted the Packers in the second round of the NFC playoffs before a raucous (what else?) crowd at Lincoln Financial Field. The winner would move on to the NFC Championship Game and have a chance to play in the Super Bowl.

It was a game that pitted two good teams playing at their peak. Two old friends, Andy Reid for the Eagles and Mike Sherman for the Packers, were the coaches, and two quarterbacks—Green Bay's Brett Favre and Philly's Donovan McNabb—were playing superbly.

The Packers took command early, leading 14–0 after one quarter because of two Favre touchdown passes. The Eagles cut into the deficit in the second quarter on a touchdown toss to Duce Staley.

On the first play of the fourth quarter, the Eagles tied the game when McNabb threw a touchdown pass to Todd Pinkston, but

Green Bay roared right back, getting a Ryan Longwell field goal that seemed to all but put away the game 17–14.

Then it started.

Beginning their final drive on their own 22, the Eagles sputtered from the beginning. After a 22-yard run by Staley, McNabb first threw incomplete, and then the Eagles were penalized five yards. On the next play, McNabb was sacked for a 16-yard loss back to his 25, and then a third-down pass fell incomplete.

This was it. The Eagles faced fourth-and-26, and if they could not convert, the game was over and the team would have another playoff failure to contemplate.

Let it be understood that coaches have very few plays drawn up to convert 26 yards with any regularity. Reid called 74 Double Go, a play basically designed to go down the middle for wide receiver Freddie Mitchell.

Mitchell had been upset throughout the game because McNabb had not thrown him a pass, and in the huddle before the play, the quarterback looked at the receiver and asked simply, "You ready?"

Mitchell said, "I've been ready the whole game."

McNabb received the snap from the shotgun formation just before the 35-second clock expired and, after eluding a rush, he rocketed a pass down the middle to Mitchell, who inexplicably found himself in a gap in the Packers defense.

Linebacker Nick Barnett had not dropped deep enough, safety Darren Sharper was too deep, and young cornerback Bhawoh Jue was late getting to the middle of the field. Mitchell snagged the pass and was blasted. He needed 26 yards, and he got 28. The crowd went crazy.

The Eagles moved the ball just far enough against the stunned Packers defense for David Akers to convert a 37-yard field goal to tie the game and send it into overtime. In OT Eagles safety Brian Dawkins intercepted Favre, and Akers stepped up to kick a 31-yard field goal that won the game.

For the Eagles, it was the kind of improbable good fortune that usually went to their opponents in the postseason. Unfortunately, they couldn't sustain it and were beaten by the Carolina Panthers in the NFC Championship Game.

What happened with the Packers was even more interesting. Though no one chose to point any fingers about the late-game collapse, Sherman fired defensive coordinator Ed Donatell a few days later.

Mitchell, a first-round draft pick in 2001 who had so far done nothing, lived off that catch for a while, nicknaming himself "Fourth-and-26 Freddie." But he was gone after the next season.

Nonetheless, among Eagles fans, that conversion usually ranks among the top two or three plays in team history.

40 Earle "Greasy" Neale

There is a special place in Eagles lore for the guy they called "Greasy." No one for sure knows where the nickname truly originated, though two stories seem to have stood the test of time.

One says that it came from his high school football coach in West Virginia, who said Earle Neale was so elusive when trying to be tackled that he was greasy. The second goes back even further when, as a kid during a name-calling session with a classmate, Neale called the other kid "dirty." That kid, trying to one-up him, called Neale "greasy."

So take your pick on the genesis of one of the great names in sports history. But this much is not the subject of speculation: Neale was the first great coach in Eagles history, and he could not have come at a better time.

When Neale was named head coach in 1941, the Eagles had been a member of the NFL for eight seasons but had yet to enjoy a winning season under two different coaches—first Lud Wray and then team founder and owner Bert Bell. Had Neale not brought the quality of Philly pro football up several notches, including trips to three straight NFL Championship Games and two championships, who knows what the fate of the franchise might have been? But Neale was the right man at the right time, and he brought with him a revolutionary new offense that changed the course of the Philadelphia Eagles.

Neale came to football coaching relatively late after spending eight seasons in pro baseball playing for the Cincinnati Reds. In fact, he was a member of the Reds team that beat the infamous Chicago White Sox in the 1919 World Series. Of course, that was the series in which the powerful White Sox were accused of losing on purpose and receiving payoffs from gamblers. The players always denied it and, in a sensational trial, were ultimately acquitted. Neale insisted to his dying day that the series was played on the level.

But after baseball, he went into college football coaching at Washington and Jefferson College, Virginia, West Virginia, and Yale before Eagles owner Lex Thompson contacted him in 1941. By then, the Eagles were already an NFL laughingstock, having posted a 19–65–3 record in their first eight seasons.

Neale, a relentlessly organized man, wasted no time going to work. And his first task was to analyze the T-formation offense run by the Chicago Bears, who had just beaten Washington 73–0 in the NFL Championship Game. He took the best of the offense and then improved it, most dramatically adding more deceptive ball-handling by the quarterback.

"He was the smartest football man I ever met," said Tommy Thompson, the Eagles' quarterback at the time. "His memory was fantastic." He could remember what teams had done against him months and years before and find ways to combat it.

"He was the best coach I ever played for," linebacker Chuck Bednarik said.

After two more subpar seasons, it began to come together, ironically, with the so-called Steagles in 1943.

In 1944, again as just the Eagles, Philly had its first winning season, going 7–1–2 and finishing second in the division behind the New York Giants. But by this stage, Neale was getting the players he needed to make a move forward. He had running back Steve Van Buren, two-way star Al Wistert, Thompson, and others, and now the offense he envisioned could take flight.

Over the next two seasons, the Eagles continued to develop and mature, posting seasons of 7–3 and 6–5 before finally breaking through in 1947. Using the talents of recently signed Pete Pihos, Neale developed the Pihos Screen, a forerunner of today's screen pass that made life miserable for opposing defenses.

The Eagles won a franchise-best eight games that season and made it to the NFL Championship Game for the first time, where they fell 28–21 to the Chicago Cardinals.

Then came the 1948 and 1949 seasons, when everything came together and the Eagles won their first two NFL titles—first beating the Cardinals in 1948 and following it up with a victory over the Los Angeles Rams the next season.

Injuries to key players, including Van Buren, slowed the Eagles in 1950, and they fell to 6–6, the first time the Eagles did not have a winning season since 1942. But that wasn't the worst of it. After a lethargic November loss to the New York Giants, team owner James Clark stormed into the locker room afterward and publicly berated Neale. Never one to back down, Neale went nose to nose with the guy who signed his paycheck while a stunned team watched.

Two days later at practice, Clark apologized and, at least according to Neale, told him, "You can coach this team forever for me." It didn't quite work out that way.

After the season, Neale was on vacation in Florida when he received a telegram from Clark that said he'd been fired. "It was a compete surprise," said Neale, who added that the move so upset his wife that she died two months later, though no one really knows if it was related.

Coach Earle "Greasy" Neale, right, signs a new contract with the Eagles for three years on February 2, 1949. With him is president of the Eagles, Jim Clarke.

But this much was true: the most successful and longest-tenured coach in team history was gone—just like that. And it was something the franchise did not recover from for decades. "Greasy was a football genius," Bednarik said. "What happened to him was a tragedy."

His record over 10 seasons was 63–43–5, and he led the Eagles to three NFL East titles. His victory total stood for years until Andy Reid recently broke it.

He retired to Florida after that and was inducted into the Pro Football Hall of Fame in 1969. He died in 1973 at the age of 81.

In 1989, the Earle "Greasy" Neale Award, presented by the Maxwell Football Club, was started to honor coaches who had done the most outstanding job of working with the talent available.

And no one did that better that Greasy.

1948 NFL Championship Game

It is not generally remembered as one of the great "weather" games in NFL history, and it certainly doesn't rank with the famous Ice Bowl from 1967 when the Green Bay Packers beat the Dallas Cowboys in temperatures hovering around 20 below.

But make no mistake, when the Eagles faced the Chicago Cardinals on December 19, 1948, in Shibe Park in the NFL Championship Game, the weather was the first and last topic of conversation. Except, of course, for the fact that the Eagles won and collected their first-ever NFL title.

There was nothing pretty about this one, which was a rematch of the previous season's title game, won 28–21 by the Cardinals, in the bitter cold of Chicago's Comiskey Park. The Eagles left that game steaming, convinced they were the better team but having made too many mistakes to take advantage of what they felt was their superiority.

So when the two teams met again in 1948, the Eagles' opinion hadn't changed. "We respected the Cardinals," All-Pro two-way star Al Wistert said. "But we felt confident we could beat them. We knew we were better."

The Eagles rolled into the title game after posting a 9–2–1 record and featuring a roster of stars including quarterback Tommy Thompson, running back Steve Van Buren, tight end Pete Pihos, and Wistert. And while the Eagles dominated just about everyone they faced that season, one of their two losses came in the season opener against the Cardinals.

That loss to the Cards, as well as the one the previous season in the title game, had Eagles coach Greasy Neale seeing red and ready for revenge. "It was a pride thing with him," Wistert said. "He knew we were better."

And when the chance came to play them again for the championship, Neale was thrilled and was even happier when he learned his Eagles, despite playing at home, were underdogs. "No one believes in you," he said every day after practice. "Show everybody." "Greasy really had us keyed up," Wistert said.

All things being equal, Neale liked his team's chances. But the night before the game, a major winter snowstorm rolled into town. It started around dawn and continued all day. Nicknamed the "Philly Blizzard," by the time it was done that night, it had dumped nearly 20 inches of snow on the city.

The morning of the game, as the storm howled, Neale thought it might make more sense to postpone the game, and NFL commissioner Bert Bell decided to leave the decision up to the two teams. Neale checked with the Cardinals, and they wanted to play. Neale returned to the Philadelphia locker room, where the Eagles had voted they wanted to play as well. He said, "Can you believe it? They want to play. Let's go beat the hell out of them!"

Despite the weather, nearly 28,000 fans showed up for the game, most if them walking in because nearly every road leading to the stadium was all but impassable.

The players from both teams helped the Shibe Park grounds crew remove the snow-laden tarp from the field because it was simply too heavy for them to handle. Once the covering was removed, the snow began piling up to the point where yard lines were obliterated. Referee Ron Gibbs was responsible for all down and distance decisions because the lines were not visible, both teams agreed not to challenge an official's spot of the ball, and there were no measurements taken. Why bother?

Van Buren said the conditions looked a lot worse than they actually ended up being. "The footing wasn't that bad," he said. "The only problem was seeing. It was snowing so hard I couldn't even see their safety."

The game itself was what you might expect from two teams playing in a raging blizzard. Both teams knew they would probably accomplish very little offensively and it would be a mistake that would decide the game. And that's exactly what happened.

The game was scoreless late in the third quarter when Eagles linemen Bucko Kilroy and Alex Wojciechowicz hit Chicago quarterback Ray Mallouf and forced a fumble, which Kilroy recovered at the Cardinals' 17-yard line. Three plays into the fourth quarter, Van Buren went almost untouched into the end zone from five yards out. "It was one of the easiest touchdowns I ever scored," Van Buren said.

It was the first, last, and only score of the day, and it was enough to bring an NFL championship to Philadelphia for the first time in the club's 16-year history.

"We worked so hard, and finally the reward was there," Van Buren said. "Even old Greasy was choked up."

1949 NFL Championship Game

Winning a championship says one thing. Winning two in a row says something else entirely. Two in a row establishes a pattern. It makes it clear that a team isn't some flash in the pan who got lucky one season. It says *continuity*, and it says *talent*. And if the word had existed for sports teams in the 1940s, it might well have said *dynasty*.

So it was in Philadelphia in the late 1940s. They were a cast of true characters, many of whom had been toughened by the horror of World War II just a few years earlier. Many had served in combat and had learned what sacrifice really was. That meant gaining three yards with a football game on the line was mere child's play.

These were tough, tough guys who played both offense and defense, rarely left the field, and played through the kinds of injuries that would leave players today on the injured reserve list. They did it because, well, that's what you did to be successful. And they played for not a lot of money because they loved the game. The Eagles had more than their share of these types of players, and that was one of the reasons they fought through a blizzard to win their first NFL title.

Now as the 1949 season loomed, the Eagles faced an even tougher task: doing it again. Only one team in league history, the 1940–41 Bears, had won two championship games in a row, but the Eagles saw no reason why they shouldn't be the second team to do so. Everyone from the 1948 title team was back, as was their coach Greasy Neale, and the Eagles got lucky by landing a player in the draft that they knew was going to be a star immediately—a rock-hard kid from Penn named Chuck Bednarik.

"We were an awesome team," team captain and All-Pro tackle Al Wistert said. Indeed, if the Eagles were very good in 1948, they were nearly unstoppable in 1949, rolling to an 11–1 record and outscoring their opposition 364–134. Their only loss was a 38–21 loss to the Bears in the fourth week of the season. From that point on, they were barely challenged.

In fact, the Eagles barely broke a sweat in winning the Eastern Division title. All they waited for to establish what they hoped would be their enduring legacy was to see who they would face in the NFL Championship Game.

Their title foe from the previous two seasons—the Chicago Cardinals—fell back in the standings, and the Chicago Bears, who had beaten the Eagles 12 of the last 13 times they'd met (including that season), missed out on the division title by a mere half game to the Los Angeles Rams, who finished 8–2–2.

The biggest struggle the Eagles faced was getting out to the West Coast for the game that was scheduled for December 18, 1949. It ended up being a three-day trip by train, though the train did stop every day for an hour to allow the Eagles to practice.

"It was terrible," Bednarik recalled. "We'd practice for an hour in an open field somewhere, and the rest of the passengers would wait until we were done. Then we'd get back on, and the train would start again. That's how we prepared for a world championship game. Can you believe it?"

Few of the players could sleep either because of the rocking of the train, so when they finally arrived in Los Angeles, they were exhausted and testy.

Game day finally arrived at the Los Angeles Coliseum and, one more time, the Eagles came face to face with horrendous weather. It had been a blizzard the year before in Philadelphia, but this time it was torrential, unceasing rain that began on Saturday and continued all day Sunday.

And while fans in Philly were a hardy bunch and showed up for the championship game the year before in Philly despite the snow and wind, L.A. fans weren't quite so fanatical. The Coliseum seated 100,000 fans, and officials expected more than 75,000 attend. But the weather was so bad, by California standards at least, that barely 28,000 actually showed up.

And for the second straight year, commissioner Bert Bell considered postponing the game. This time the Eagles voted to postpone, but not because of any safety issues. For the Eagles, it was strictly a financial decision because they knew the better the attendance, the more money each player would receive. But Bell was unsympathetic and ordered the game played.

Both teams took the field, which better resembled a mud pit. Players were ankle-deep in mud and could get no traction whatsoever. Most players said the field in Los Angeles was worse than the one they had played on at Shibe Park the year before.

One of the few players unaffected by the conditions was the ubiquitous Steve Van Buren. Already known as the perhaps the top back in football, he received extra motivation from what he considered dirty play by the Rams early in the game. On one play, Van Buren was knocked out of bounds and hit late by a Rams player, and one of them came up to Van Buren and said, "We're going to kill you, Steve."

That angered the mild-mannered Van Buren, who went back to the huddle and told quarterback Tommy Thompson to keep giving him the ball. Thompson complied, and Van Buren made NFL history.

On as lousy a field as he'd ever played on, Van Buren ran for what was then an NFL Championship Game–record 196 yards on 31 carries. That record stood for 38 years until the Washington Redskins' Timmy Smith ran for 204 yards in Super Bowl XXII.

The Eagles carved out two touchdowns—a 31-yard pass from Thompson to Pete Pihos and a blocked punt and recovery in the end zone by rookie Leo Skladany. That's all the Eagles needed to secure their second-straight world title. They are still the only team to win back-to-back NFL titles by shutout.

In a "celebration" later, the Eagles' conglomerate of owners called the "100 Brothers" didn't pull out all the stops. Players were simply awarded cigarette lighters—which weren't even engraved. "A cigarette lighter for winning two straight world championships," a bemused Wistert said.

All good things eventually come to an end, and so it was with the high-flying Eagles. Van Buren was slowed by injuries, the inevitable complacency began to seep in, and the Eagles fell to 6–6 in 1950, losing their last four games along the way.

The Eagles would not win another world title until 1960, but the legacy of those teams from the late 1940s will never be forgotten.

"We won two straight," Wistert said. "Not too many people can say that."

43 1947 NFL Championship Game

Championship teams have to start somewhere. And the Philadelphia Eagles began their remarkable streak of three straight appearances in the NFL Championship Game in 1947.

Despite some early failures under head coach Greasy Neale, by 1947 the pieces appeared to be in place for a legitimate championship run. The Eagles had traded for top-notch offensive lineman Alex Wojciechowicz the year before and drafted fullback Joe Muha and halfback Russ Craft. They already had Steve Van Buren, a star back in the making, and they also added tight end Pete Pihos. All they needed was the opportunity. It finally arrived in 1947. The Eagles put together their fourth-straight winning season, going 8–4 after beating the Green Bay Packers in the season finale.

But there were no tiebreakers or point differentials or head-to-head performances back then. The Eagles tied the Pittsburgh Steelers for the best record in the East, and the only way to break that tie was to play each other. So the two teams met December 21 at Forbes Field in Pittsburgh. In truth, it was never a contest.

Quarterback Tommy Thompson threw touchdown passes to Van Buren and Jack Ferrante, and Bosh Pritchard returned a punt 79 yards for another score in a dominating 21–0 win. For the Eagles, it was their first-ever playoff victory (because, in truth, that's what it was) and it set up a chance for them to play for their first NFL title.

What awaited them was another team that had struggled for NFL relevance during its history. The Chicago Cardinals had always played second fiddle to the more popular Bears. While the Bears played their home games at Wrigley Field, the Cardinals were relegated to the South Side to play at Comiskey Park.

"We didn't get the crowds at Comiskey Park that the Bears got at Wrigley Field," former Cardinals center and linebacker Vince Banonis said. "All the rich people were on the North Side, and we got the leftovers."

Still, the Cardinals forged a 9–3 record, made even sweeter by the fact that they beat the hated Bears 30–21 in the season finale to secure the Western Division title.

The Eagles would also play in Chicago, where the weather would torment both teams. Again, no one knew it at the time, but lousy weather would plague the Eagles in all three of their trips to the NFL Championship Game. This time it was a frozen field brought on by 20-degree temperatures and sleet. None of the players on either side could get a decent grip on the football, and Van Buren complained that he slipped twice just coming out of the huddle. The Eagles wore sneakers to try to get some traction, while the Cardinals wore custom-designed cleats that handled the surface better.

And while the Eagles had Van Buren, one of the top backs in the league, the Cardinals had a pretty good back of their own in Charley Trippi. Trippi scored one touchdown on a 44-yard run and a second on a 75-yard punt return, while Elmer Angsman had a 70-yard scoring run to take a 21–7 lead.

The Eagles hung around and played well but never could get the one play they needed and, in their first experience in the NFL Championship Game, they fell 28–21. The game wasn't put away, though, until Chicago's Marshall Goldberg intercepted a Thompson pass late in the game.

In many ways, Philly outplayed the Cardinals as Thompson completed 27 of 44 passes for 297 yards; the completions and yardage were both NFL Championship Game records. Also, the Eagles outgained the Cardinals in overall yardage, 357 to 336.

But Trippi was the difference, piling up 206 total yards, including 102 on two punt returns. Meanwhile, Van Buren never could gain his footing, and the Eagles managed just 60 yards on the ground.

It was a bittersweet conclusion to what had been a great season for the Eagles. They knew it was just the beginning and used the loss as a springboard to win championships the next two seasons.

For the Cardinals, it was the beginning of the end. After losing the 1948 NFL Championship Game to the Eagles, they never had a return to glory. By the mid-1950s, the Cardinals were among the NFL's doormats and, after the 1959 season, seeing that they couldn't compete with the bankroll or the popularity of the rival Bears, the team was relocated to St. Louis.

Norm Snead

Norm Snead never seemed to catch a break. A talented quarterback and a terrific guy, he was the victim of bad timing and worse football and never really got the credit he deserved as a quality NFL quarterback. In his 16-year career, Snead threw for nearly 31,000 yards and 196 touchdowns while also heaving 257 interceptions. In that same period, he managed to play on winning teams in just three of those seasons—the 1966 Eagles, the 1971 Minnesota Vikings, and the 1972 New York Giants. He was a good player stuck on bad teams.

And while Snead played much of his career in other uniforms, he is best known as an Eagle and had some of his best years in Philadelphia. But it was never easy for the guy they called "Norman."

He came out of Wake Forest University as the No. 1 draft pick of the sorry Washington Redskins. In his three seasons as the starter, the Skins were just 9–30–3 and Snead completed fewer than half of his passes and was intercepted 71 times while throwing just 46 touchdown passes.

Then came the 1964 seasons and the arrival of Joe Kuharich as Philly's head coach and general manager. One of his first acts was to go through what amounted to a yard sale. He dealt popular, productive players like Tommy McDonald, Lee Roy Caffey, and Clarence Peaks for players no one really knew that much about.

And as unpopular as those deals were, the one that really sent Eagles fan over the edge was the trading of up-and-coming star quarterback Sonny Jurgensen to the Redskins for Snead. As a result, Snead received brutal treatment from Eagles fans, and nothing he did was ever good enough to them.

But years later, Snead still insists he never took any of it personally. "I thought the fans in Philly were great," he said. "They were a lot like fans anywhere. If you played badly and the team lost, they booed. But if you played well, they let you know they appreciated it. Philadelphia is a passionate sports city. Nobody likes to get booed, but it's not personal. At least I never viewed it as personal."

Snead was the main quarterback his first two years in Philly and played OK. But in 1966, Snead was embroiled in Kuharich's grand experiment to play three quarterbacks—Snead, King Hill, and Jack Concannon—on a rotating basis. Snead was furious but went along and, in the end, the system produced the first winning season of his NFL career.

In 1967 Kuharich ended the experiment by trading Concannon to the Chicago Bears and making Snead his No. 1 guy. Snead responded with the best season of his career, throwing for a career-high 3,399 yards and 29 touchdowns.

But in 1968, he broke his leg in a preseason game, and nothing was ever quite the same. He threw a league-high 21 interceptions that season and followed it up with another NFL-worst 23 interceptions the next season. In 1970 he threw 15 touchdown passes and another 20 interceptions, and after that season he was dealt to the Minnesota Vikings for three draft picks and a backup tackle.

Coach Jerry Williams admitted that even though Snead departed as the Eagles' all-time leader in several categories—including pass attempts, pass completions, passing yards, touchdowns, and interceptions—the quarterback needed a change of venue. "The fans' negative attitude toward Norman played a role in our decision," he said. "Hopefully this move will prove beneficial to everybody."

Snead played one season for the Vikings, lost his starting job at midseason to Bob Lee, and was dealt again, this time to the New York Giants. Then, two years later, he was traded to the 49ers and then, finally, he was picked back up by the Giants, where he ended his career in 1976 at age 37.

Snead's numbers were comparable to many NFL quarterbacks of the day, including Hall of Famers like Y.A. Tittle and Bart Starr, but his record as a starting quarterback was a depressing 52–99–7.

But Snead would have changed none of it—especially his years in Philadelphia. "It's a shame we never put it together in Philadelphia," he said. "It seemed like we were right on the verge a few times, then one or two guys would go down with injuries. But I enjoyed my time there."

Just maybe, Eagles fans will one day give Norman Snead the break and the respect he always deserved.

45 The Trade

For years, Eagles fans knew of just one trade that rocked the organization to its foundation: sending starting quarterback Sonny Jurgensen to the Redskins for Norm Snead in 1964. It was a deal Eagles fans howled about for years and, frankly, still howl about today. But that all changed on Easter Sunday in 2010.

On that day, the Eagles dramatically cut the ties with their past and focused on an uncertain future when they sent their starting quarterback of the past 11 years, Donovan McNabb, to the Washington Redskins for a second-round draft pick in the 2010 draft and either a third- or fourth-round selection in 2011.

And while rumors had swirled for weeks of a possible blockbuster Eagles trade, few really thought it would involve the record-setting and longest-tenured quarterback in team history. For many Eagles fans, McNabb was the face of the franchise, and few could remember a time when he wasn't under center. But circumstances—including McNabb's contract issues, the growth of backup Kevin Kolb, and the potential of No. 3 quarterback Michael Vick—suddenly made McNabb expendable.

And while everyone involved said all the right things, there was clearly a strain underneath the good words. After all, the Eagles did what few pro teams in any sport would do—they traded a key player to a team within the same division. That meant McNabb would face his old team twice a season, but it also said that the Eagles weren't all that concerned about it.

McNabb had never wanted to leave Philadelphia. He was happy, established, and still convinced he could perform for the Eagles. His résumé suggested that too. From 2000 to 2009, with McNabb at the helm, the Eagles had won an NFC-best 103 regular-season games and nine playoff games. They also had five division titles, three trips to the NFC Championship Game, and a berth in the Super Bowl.

But that strength was also McNabb's weakness. There was the perception, real or not, that he could not win the big game when it mattered most. And even a year earlier, there were questions about how much gas McNabb, at age 33, had left in the tank.

Whatever the real reason, events moved quickly after the end of the 2009 season, when the Eagles went 11–5 and were ousted in the first round of the playoffs by the Dallas Cowboys. That season, McNabb threw for 3,553 yards and 22 touchdowns in 14 games, but he played poorly in the regular-season finale, a loss to the Cowboys that cost the Eagles the division title and a first-round playoff bye. He played even worse the following week, this time a 34–14 loss to the Cowboys in the postseason.

After the game, Reid insisted McNabb would be back in 2010 and repeated that several times during the off-season. But it was also clear that if the right offer came, the Eagles would entertain it. And in late March, events moved even quicker, especially when new Redskins coach and general manager Mike Shanahan got involved.

Seeing the handwriting on the wall, McNabb issued a statement saying he wanted to remain an Eagle but understood if the team had to make a deal.

On April 4, Easter Sunday, McNabb got the word that he had been traded to the Redskins for the two draft picks. He could have let the Eagles have it with both barrels but chose not to. He took the high road for the sake of both organizations and himself. "I'm really excited about my future with the Washington Redskins," he said in a statement. "I'm eager to work with Coach Shanahan. He's been a very successful coach with a couple of Super Bowl victories on his résumé. While it has been my goal to win a Super Bowl in Philadelphia, we came up short. I enjoyed my 11 years and know we shared a lot more good times than bad." It was a classy way to depart.

Reid defended the decision, which split Eagles fans nearly right down the middle: Some thought it was time for a change, and still others believed McNabb was still the guy who could get the job done. "I can't deny there wasn't a choice to be made," Reid said. "There were things offered for Kevin [Kolb], but I thought this was the best deal. This happened to be the best deal for everybody. This was a very tough decision."

McNabb left Philadelphia as a six-time Pro Bowler and the franchise's all-time leader in passing yards (32,873), completions (2,801), attempts (4,746), completion percentage (59), and touchdown passes (216). He also rushed for another 3,249 yards (ninth-best in team history) and 28 touchdowns.

In Washington, however, it could not have ended much worse for McNabb after a promising start. He led the Skins to a season-opening win over the Cowboys and, in an overtime loss to Houston, threw for 426 yards in Week 2.

But by midseason, the combination of McNabb and the Redskins offense was not working. McNabb was benched in the final minute of a loss to the Lions because, as Shanahan put it afterward, McNabb still didn't have a complete grasp of the offense. It was an embarrassing episode that stayed with McNabb the rest of the season. Then, with three weeks left in another awful season, Shanahan benched McNabb for the rest of the season in favor of journeyman Rex Grossman.

McNabb threw for 3,377 yards but only had 14 touchdowns to go with 15 interceptions. McNabb again tried to stay positive, but it became obvious after the season that he likely would be traded again. Faced with that prospect, McNabb just smiled and said, "I know I can still play."

46 Miracle at the Meadowlands II

For a new generation of Eagles fans, this was their seminal moment. As it was for an older generation 30 years earlier, these fans knew exactly where they were and what they were doing when a miracle struck in the swamps of southern New Jersey on December 19, 2010.

While the old folks had their Herman Edwards and Joe Pisarcik and Larry Csonka from 1978, the kids had DeSean Jackson, Matt Dodge, and Tom Coughlin. Both games had incredible finishes. Both games featured bone-headed decisions. And both games will never be forgotten. "Just unbelievable," said New York Giants quarterback Eli Manning.

But this was Giants-Eagles, so maybe it was all too believable.

As real Eagles fans always recall, this was actually the *third* Miracle at the Meadowlands. In October 2003 Brian Westbrook returned a punt 84 yards for a touchdown with just over a minute to play to pull out an improbable 14–10 win. But that one lacked the jaw-dropping quality of Edwards' fumble recovery for the game-winning touchdown in the final seconds in 1978.

And when DeSean Jackson returned a Giants' punt 65 yards on the game's last play in 2010, the attitude was much the same—disbelief bordering on stupefaction. How could such a thing happen? There are some people who are still asking that question.

Of course, everyone remembers the final, spine-tingling play by Jackson and the baffled, stunned look on Giants coach Tom Coughlin's face afterward. But the fact is, the Eagles rallied from 21 points down to win the game 38–31 and are the only team in NFL history to come back from 21 points down with less than eight minutes to play to win in regulation.

The victory sent the Eagles toward the NFC East title, and the loss sent the Giants spiraling. They had led the division most of the season, but that loss was a death knell, and they missed the playoffs altogether. "We sent out a message that we're a heck of a team," Philly running back LeSean McCoy said. "Don't get too comfortable with a lead because we're coming back."

But there would have been no miracle if the Eagles hadn't put themselves in a position to create one. Midway through the final quarter, the Giants were well in command of a 31–10 lead. But Michael Vick connected with Brent Celek for a 65-yard touchdown with 7:28 to play to cut the deficit to 31–17. The Giants failed to do anything with the ball on their next possession, and Vick led another drive, this time capping it with a four-yard scoring run with 5:28 left to make the score 31–24.

One more drive resulted in one more score, this time with Vick throwing 13 yards to Jeremy Maclin for the tying touchdown. For the Giants and their dazed fans in their new stadium, that was bad enough. But it was about to get a lot worse.

Jackson, one the game's most dangerous punt returners, had been hobbled due to a foot injury and wasn't sure if he'd even play that day. And he certainly wasn't planning to return any kicks. But Reid asked him if he could go, and Jackson said yes. So in the final seconds of a game that figured to go to overtime, Jackson planted himself at the Eagles 35-yard line and waited.

"Honestly, I was sitting back there thinking to myself, *They're really not going to kick to me, they're going to kick it out of bounds,*" Jackson said after the game. And, in truth, that was the Giants' plan and the last thing Coughlin told his rookie punter, Matt Dodge. But Dodge said later the snap was high, and it threw off is timing. Instead, he sent a tailor-made line-drive kick to Jackson in the middle of the field.

Jackson dropped the ball, picked it up, found a crease to the right, and was gone. For the final 30 yards, no one was close to Jackson and, as the game clock went toward all zeroes, he slowed down to make sure the Giants would have no time to do anything. At the end, he dove into the end zone in celebration. "It was a dream come true," Jackson said.

The stadium was silent as a tomb except for the celebrating Eagles. Giants players stood staring, hands on hips or looking down in complete disbelief.

Coughlin found his shaken punter and kept asking him, "What were you doing? What were you doing?"

The Eagles were no doubt as shocked as the Giants. "I've never been a part of anything like this before," Celek said.

And it's a play that has found its way comfortably, and for all time, on to the list of greatest plays in team history.

47 Brian Dawkins

On December 28, 2008 Brian Dawkins knew something was different. He knew when he stepped on the frozen turf of the Linc to face his ancient rival, the Dallas Cowboys, in the regular-season finale that this very well could be the last time he played in front of what he considered the greatest fans in the world.

"I had to calm myself down," the Eagles veteran safety told the *Newark Star-Ledger*. That's because so much was at play that afternoon. Not only was Dawkins thinking that he'd be leaving the only NFL home he'd known after 13 seasons, he also knew the Eagles needed to beat the Cowboys to keep their playoff hopes alive.

And in a performance Eagles fans and teammates had come to expect, when the stage was largest, Dawkins was at his best. Dawkins forced two fumbles, both of which were returned for touchdowns, to help catapult the Eagles to a decisive 44–6 win. The Eagles would reach the playoffs and beat the Vikings and Giants on the road before falling to the Arizona Cardinals in the NFC Championship Game.

A month later, Dawkins signed a five-year, $17 million free-agent deal with the Denver Broncos, and his remarkable career with the Eagles was over. But he left an indelible impression.

"If I'm going to build a football team, Brian Dawkins is my free safety," said Jim Johnson, the Eagles' late defensive coordinator, who used Dawkins as a weapon anytime and anywhere on the field. "Brian could play strong safety, corner, free safety, and not miss a beat."

Dawkins was a second-round draft pick out of Clemson for the Eagles in the 1996 draft and, before he strapped on a helmet professionally, he already had a reputation as a physical, aggressive player. "He hits like a linebacker," teammate Jeremiah Trotter said. "He hurts people."

And though Dawkins insisted he never tried to intentionally hurt anyone, he also made it clear that if you were within his range, he'd make you pay. "I would challenge anyone who calls me a dirty player," he said. "But I play hard, and sometimes things happen." It was that attitude that endeared him to fans and especially to Johnson, who would use him in every blitz package he could think of.

And Dawkins, who took over as a starter early in his rookie season, would go on to establish himself as one of the most durable players in team history. In fact, he held the team record for most games played (183), breaking the mark of 180 set by Harold Carmichael, until it was broken by David Akers in 2010. He was a seven-time Pro Bowler, was named All-Pro seven times, and is just the 10th member of the 20 interceptions/20 sacks club, and his 34 career interceptions is tied for the most in team history. In 2002, against the Houston Texans, Dawkins was also the first player in league history to record a sack, an interception, force a fumble, and catch a touchdown pass in the same game.

The Eagles knew they might not be able to retain his services after the 2008 season and, when Dawkins left, it created a gaping hole in Philly's secondary. Worse, Dawkins went to Denver and was named to his eighth Pro Bowl in 2009.

His 2010 season was complicated by injuries, and he played only 11 games. In 2011, he came back for another season with the Broncos, playing in 14 games and earning another Pro Bowl berth But after that season and fulfilling his plan to retire before injuries made that decision for him, Dawkins walked away from football. There were many people in Philadelphia, including former teammates, who hoped Dawkins would be able to end his career as it started and where he belongs—with the Eagles. And that's exactly

Brian Dawkins reacts after making an interception against the Houston Texans in the third quarter of a September 29, 2002, game in Philly.

what happened as Dawkins signed a one-day contract with the Eagles in April 2012 and officially retired as a Eagle. Five months later, in a home game against the Giants, Dawkins' No. 20 was retired by the team, just the ninth number in team history to earn that honor. He returned to the team in an official capacity in 2016 as football operations director and in February 2018 was elected to the Pro Football Hall of Fame.

48 Training Camps

No one really knows—for a scientific fact, that is—where the idea of NFL training camps really came from. The prevailing wisdom (such as it is) is that Green Bay's Curly Lambeau, looking for a getaway from fans and their prying eyes, decided to take his team an hour so north of town so his Packers could practice in relative peace and quiet.

Others insist Chicago Bears founder and coach George Halas started the practice. There are even those who insist when Bert Bell took his new team—the Philadelphia Eagles—to the New Jersey Shore for their first practices that it was beginning of the training camp as we know it. But in the end, whoever started it and for whatever reason, it has become as much a part of the NFL landscape as training-camp holdouts.

Certainly the concept has changed since it first started. Back in the old days, a training camp was just that—it was six weeks of intensive, grueling practice to get players back in shape for the season to come.

Back then, though, the players needed that time. Most, if not all, held second jobs in the off-season, and most of them didn't exactly stick to a training regimen. They drank, they smoked, they ate too much, and by the time football season loomed, their paunches told them it was time to get back to work.

Of course, in the last 20 years, players have understood that there is no off-season. They train rigorously on their own, and when training camp does begin, players are expected to be in great shape. Today, training camp is more like fine-tuning what has already been installed in earlier minicamps.

The Eagles are no different from nearly every other team in the league today. Their players come to camp in late July ready to work and with an understanding of what's expected of them. In fact, training camp has become more an event for fans than the players themselves. Most camps, including the Eagles', offer special meet-the-player sessions, intrasquad scrimmages, and special autograph sessions. But in the end, it's still about getting ready for another season.

In their history, few teams have trained at more sites than the Eagles. It started with their first two seasons in Atlantic City, New Jersey, followed by a season at Chestnut Academy in Philadelphia and two seasons at Temple University. After that, the Eagles trained one season at West Chester State Teachers College in West Chester, Pennsylvania, a season at Philly's St. Joseph's University, another season at West Chester, and then the 1941 and 1942 seasons in, of all places, Two Rivers, Wisconsin.

The journey continued over the next eight years with stops in such spots as West Chester again as well as three seasons in Saranac Lake, New York, and Grand Rapids, Minnesota, before finally finding some stability in 1951 at Hershey, Pennsylvania.

The Eagles trained there until 1968, when they went to Reading's Albright College for five summers followed by Widener University in Chester from 1973 to 1979 and then back to West Chester from 1980 to 1995.

By that point, the Eagles began to understand just how significant it was to have a training spot that not only provided seclusion but convenience and, yes, a chance to generate some income.

The Eagles hadn't necessarily been unhappy at West Chester University, which was located just west of the Philly metropolitan area. But rumors began to circulate in February 1996 that owner Jeffrey Lurie wanted to move camp to Lehigh University in Bethlehem, Pennsylvania, about 50 miles north. It was a little farther away, but it opened up another market for potential season-ticket buyers, a claim Lurie also denied.

Lurie denied the reports, but in March the Eagles in fact made a deal with the university to move the Eagles camp to the Lehigh Valley. "We do not have, nor have we had, anything negative to say about West Chester and the way we were treated there," said Joe Banner, the Eagles' vice president of administration. "Quite the contrary, we had a good experience there."

At Lehigh, the Eagles had access to more and better practice fields, newer dormitories, and more expansive meeting rooms and classrooms. "The bottom line is, we feel the new location will help us better prepare the football team for the season," Banner told the *Philadelphia Daily News*.

In 2013, the Eagles moved training camp to Philadelphia, specifically the team's ultra-modern NovaCare Complex, where they practice during the season.

49 Adrian Burk's Seven Touchdowns

Consider this: in a seven-year NFL career, six of which were played with the Philadelphia Eagles, quarterback Adrian Burk threw 61 touchdown passes (55 of them with Philly).

In one October 17, 1954, game against the Washington Redskins, Burk threw seven of them. That's one-eighth of his *career* touchdown passes in one game, a 49–21 Eagles win over the unfortunate Redskins in D.C.'s Griffith Stadium. Amazingly, in four of his years, he didn't even throw seven touchdown passes in the entire season. But for one magical day, as part of one incredible season, it seemed every time Burk threw a pass, it ended up in the end zone.

"I'm sure people say, 'Who is that guy?'" Burk said years later. And, in truth, he wasn't a well-known figure on the NFL scene. Even as an Eagle, he wasn't the best-known player. Originally a first-round draft pick of the Baltimore Colts, he was traded to the Eagles a year later. And Burk did little to ingratiate himself with Eagles fans that first season, throwing a league-high 23 interceptions.

He then had to split playing time with Bobby Thomason the next two seasons before taking over again in 1954 and having the season of his career. And the highlight, obviously, was that October afternoon in D.C.

The game wasn't supposed to transpire that way, Burk said later. "Our game plan was to run the ball," he said. But every time the Eagles got near the goal line, Burk decided to take a shot at the end zone. None of his touchdown passes were longer than 26 yards, and three each went to ends Pete Pihos and Bobby Walston, the other going to halfback Toy Ledbetter. "It seemed like every time I threw a pass, it went for six points," Burk said.

With the Eagles well ahead in the game, coach Jim Trimble removed Burk in the fourth quarter after he had thrown six touchdowns. But Trimble was informed by publicity director Ed Hogan that Burk was just one away from tying an NFL record. Trimble sent Burk back in to relieve Thomason and told him to go for it. He did so by connecting with Pihos for the record-tying score.

Unaware what was happening at the time, Pihos said later he was glad he didn't know. "If I'd known, I probably would've dropped the damn thing," he said.

Incredibly, despite all those touchdown passes, Burk's numbers for the day were a relatively pedestrian 19 of 27 for 232 yards. For the season, Burk threw a career-best—and NFL-best—23 touchdown passes, nearly one-third of them coming that day.

Burk's performance tied an NFL record set nine years earlier by the Chicago Bears' Sid Luckman and equaled later by the Houston Oilers' George Blanda in 1961, the New York Giants' Y.A. Tittle in 1962, and the Minnesota Vikings' Joe Kapp in 1969.

After Burk retired in 1956, he went on to a successful side career as an NFL field judge and worked the game in 1969 when Kapp threw his record-tying seven touchdown passes against the Baltimore Colts. Burk died in 2003.

50 Jeffrey Lurie

Jeffrey Lurie stood in his personal box at U.S. Bank Stadium in Minneapolis and drank it all in. His Eagles had finally won the Super Bowl, and with Bradley Cooper, the Hollywood star who made no bones about his love for the Eagles, standing next to him, watched the celebration.

And it was every bit what he had expected.

Say what you will about the men who have owned the Philadelphia Eagles over the years. They have been an eclectic, interesting, immensely entertaining bunch. Whether it was the man who started it all—team founder/coach/general manager/trainer/owner Bert Bell—or millionaire playboy Lex Thompson or the volatile James Clark. Maybe it was Jerry Wolman, who loved to sit on the sideline with the players during games or the profligate Leonard Tose or the complex, infuriating Norman Braman. Every one of them left an indelible impact.

Then there's the team's current owner, Jeffrey Lurie, by far the least controversial of any Eagles owner but the man who has overseen the longest stretch of sustained success for the franchise. Coincidence? Doubtful.

Since he purchased the team from Braman in May 1994 for a staggering $185 million (though some reports put it as high as $198 million), he has watched the Eagles go to six NFC Championship Games and two Super Bowls. He has done what all owners say they'll do but rarely follow through on: he has let the coaches coach and the players play and, for the most part, he has stayed out of the way. It's a philosophy that is especially foreign in the Eagles organization, in which it seemed every owner prior to Lurie tried to do everything they could to make it clear they were in charge.

And while Lurie has had his moments when, perhaps, ego got the better of him, he learned his lesson early that the people who know football, know football.

He said when he bought the team that his sole goal was to bring a championship to Philadelphia and now, as the man who has owned the team the longest in franchise history, he has grown and matured into one of the better owners in professional sports.

Lurie was born in Boston and grew up a huge fan of all Boston sports—whether it was the Red Sox, the Celtics, or the old Boston Patriots.

In the 1940s his grandfather owned nine of the nation's 15 drive-in movie theaters and eventually spun off into conglomerates that included General Cinema Corp., insurance companies, publishing houses, and more. Into that world stepped Jeffrey Lurie, and he did very nicely for himself financially, creating Chestnut Hill Productions, a film company based in Los Angeles.

As a longtime sports fan, he always wanted to own a sports team, and in 1993 he got into a bidding war with Robert Kraft to purchase the New England Patriots. But once the price hit $150 million, Lurie dropped out. He also partnered with officials in Maryland in bring an NFL expansion team to Baltimore to fill the vacuum left years earlier by the painful departure of the Colts. But he was disappointed again when the NFL put expansion teams in Jacksonville, Florida, and Charlotte, North Carolina.

But in 1994 Lurie saw another opportunity—and maybe the best one of all. He learned that Norman Braman was looking to sell the Eagles, and Lurie let nothing stop him from purchasing the team.

And he was like a kid with a new toy. In the team's first training camp after the purchase, Lurie set up an office for himself in the West Chester dorm and often worked late to make sure nothing was missed. Quarterback Randall Cunningham was quoted as saying, "$185 million for the team and he's staying with us at the dorm. That's what you call down-to-earth."

There is also the story of when Lurie saw a rookie wearing Reggie White's old No. 92 during training camp. He went to the equipment manager and told him not to issue that number again without Lurie's permission because it was an insult to the one-time great Eagles defensive end.

When White, who was by then playing for the Green Bay Packers, heard about that, he called Lurie to thank him for the gesture. The two men, who had never met before, became fast friends. White once said to Lurie, "If you'd only bought the team a year earlier..."

Lurie also went about improving facilities, taking the lead on building the new Lincoln Financial Field to replace crumbling Veterans Stadium and developing a state-of-the-art $37 million practice facility, NovaCare, which opened in 2001 and includes indoor and outdoor practice fields, medical and training facilities, and administrative offices.

On the personnel side, he hired his buddy Joe Banner as team vice president in 1994 to help him run the team and, in turn, Banner helped put the pieces in place to help with the long-term success.

When it was time for a change, he made those moves too. He brought in Howard Roseman as the general manager and let him make the moves that needed to be made. That included signing a boatload of free agents who helped make the difference in the 2017 season. It also included the biggest move, going against conventional wisdom and hiring a relatively unknown and untested Doug Pederson as head coach.

That's not to say there haven't been missteps. After his first season as owner, Lurie fired coach Rich Kotite and, after nearly rehiring former Eagles coach Dick Vermeil, he settled on Ray Rhodes. After four seasons, including a disastrous 3–13 campaign in 1998 when the players simply tuned out their coach, he hired a relative unknown, Packers tight-ends coach Andy Reid. But when it was time for a change there, too, Reid was let go after the 2012 season.

When he arrived in 1994, he instructed his coaches to keep the best 53 players they had, even if it meant challenging the salary cap. To that end, Lurie asked six veteran players to take pay cuts. The players refused, and Lurie went ahead anyway. They took their grievance to the player's association, and the players got most of their back pay restored.

What was truly interesting was what happened after that. In the past, if an owner had been publicly embarrassed like that, he might well have taken retribution against players. Not Lurie. "I'll admit it," he said. "I made a mistake. But I just wanted to make sure we started the season with our best players. I'm going to make mistakes, but I think people will respect a well-intentioned owner."

Since then, he has rarely stuck his nose in football issues and has allowed his people to do the jobs they were hired to do.

And it all became worthwhile as he watched his team finally win the Super Bowl in 2017.

"It's always about the fans," he said. "These fans are the most passionate, most deserving fans you can imagine."

51 Tailgating Philly-Style

When the topic of which NFL city has the best tailgating experience arises, fans from every city with an NFL team believe their venue is the best. And maybe that's the way it should be.

But in truth some places are indeed better than others. Whether it's the food or the fans or the location or the weather, some NFL locations just have it over others. And one city that usually makes every list for the top tailgating experience is Philadelphia.

That brings us to a guy named Joe Cahn, who sold his New Orleans cooking school in 1996, bought a motorhome, and proceeded to tailgate at every stadium in the NFL that season. Over the years, he has continued his obsession, calling himself the "Commissioner of Tailgating" and going to more than 500 tailgating adventures in the NFL.

Along the way, he has compiled his list of the best experiences, and sitting at No. 5 is Philly's own Lincoln Financial Field. It ranked behind only Houston's Reliant Stadium, Arrowhead

Stadium in Kansas City, Ralph Wilson Stadium in Buffalo, and Green Bay's Lambeau Field.

"The Eagles fans' passion always impresses me," he told Scott Bowen of ForbesTraveler.com last year. "They might be the fans who are the most knowledgeable about their team." And, of course, Eagles fans would agree.

A tailgating adventure in Philadelphia is just that. Fans arrive, in many cases, five hours before kickoff and indulge in the kind of bacchanalia many can't even conceive of. The foods range from the predictable cheesesteaks and hoagies to macaroni and cheese to Italian fare to bratwurst to jambalaya.

Fans have figured it out. The game is secondary to the fun and camaraderie they can find in the parking lots. Indeed, hundreds of people will gather at one spot (if the food and company are really good), and that's where the party will start and—eventually—end.

And unlike many stadiums, where the party stops when the game begins, Eagles fans will return to the same spot afterward to celebrate or commiserate. But they will always have a good time.

If there is a ground zero for Eagles tailgating, it might well be Lot P next to Citizens Bank Ballpark (the Phillies' home park) on Darien Street. That's where everyone seems to gather to talk, to drink, to eat, and to have the kind of good time that comes from attending an NFL game.

Also, there are websites by the score advertising tailgating excursions not only for home games but for road trips. In fact, another poll said few NFL fans travel with their team better than the Eagles'. "This is the most passionate fan base in the NFL," former team president Joe Banner said.

Don't believe it? Just spent some time in the parking lot before a game.

52 David Akers

Other guys might have given up after the first time...the second time...the third time. David Akers, however, did not. "I knew I could kick in this league," he said.

So after failed tryouts with the Atlanta Falcons, Carolina Panthers, and a brief cup of coffee with the Washington Redskins, the free agent—who earned money as a waiter and schoolteacher while waiting for his opportunity—was ready for his close-up with the Philadelphia Eagles.

That was in 1999, when first-year head coach Andy Reid decided to give him a look as a long field-goal kicker and kickoff specialist to supplement the older Norm Johnson.

In 2000 he took over full-time kicking duties and has become one of the most accurate, reliable kickers in NFL history. Through 2010, he is a five-time Pro Bowler and the Eagles' all-time leader in points, field goals, points after touchdown, games played, and more.

Also since 2000, his 291 field goals and 1,312 points are the most of any player in the NFL. He was also named to the NFL's All-Decade Team for the 2000s.

It seems so long ago now, but Akers was what is still known around training camp as a "camp leg," a kicker with no chance of making the team but who can kick in practice to keep the regular kicker's leg fresh. And that's how it evolved in his first three NFL stops, though Akers did get a chance to kick in a game for the Redskins in 1999. He missed two long field goals and was cut.

But he got his chance in Philadelphia. Knowing he needed experience, the Eagles allocated Akers to the Berlin Thunder of the NFL's European League. He came back for the 2000 season

David Akers kicks a field goal during the Eagles' 31–17 victory over the Atlanta Falcons on October 17, 2010 in Philly.

and put a stranglehold on the job. He connected on 29 of 33 field goals, and his 121 points set a team record that he go on to break several more times.

Since taking over, his accuracy rate is 82.4 percent and, except for an injury in 2005 that forced him to miss several games, he has never scored fewer than 102 points per season for the Eagles.

But as reliable as he's been for so long, reality hit Akers and the Eagles square in the face during a January 2011 wild-card playoff game against the Packers. After falling behind early, the Eagles were rallying. But to the shock of most Eagles fans, Akers missed two second-half field goals—from 41 and 34 yards—that blunted the momentum. After the game, even Reid admitted those missed kicks were crucial.

A few days later, Akers revealed that he had spent most of the previous Friday in the hospital after it was revealed his six-year-old daughter Halley had been diagnosed with a tumor on one of her ovaries. Akers refused to use it as an excuse, but several teammates wondered aloud how he could find it in himself to even step on the field.

He earned another Pro Bowl berth for his 2010 performance, but the following season season, when he was unable to reach a contract with the Eagles, he signed a three-year, $9 million deal with the San Francisco 49ers.

And he continued to do what he always did best. He led the NFL in field goals made in 2011 (44) and helped the 49ers to the Super Bowl in 2012, but was released in the spring of 2013. He played one more season, signing with the Detroit Lions, before retiring. In 2017, he was signed on a ceremonial one-day contract, retiring as an Eagle, and in October, he was inducted into the Eagles Hall of Fame.

In his 12 seasons in Philly, he played in a club-record 188 games and still stands as the team's all-time leading scorer with 1,323 points.

"The Eagles gave me my first opportunity," Akers said of his retirement with the club. "For me, it was kind of like coming back home to a place where the fans were absolutely amazing to me and they supported me on and off the field."

53 The Linc

The official name is Lincoln Financial Field, but everyone calls it "the Linc." Opened in 2003 at a cost of $512 million, it was another of those stadiums that, according to those with the organization, had to be built.

Since 1971 Veterans Stadium had been home for the Eagles and, as spare and stark as it was when it debuted, it was even worse 30 years later. When Jeffrey Lurie purchased the team in 1994, he identified a new stadium as by far the No. 1 priority for turning the Eagles into a contender.

But there were significant roadblocks, not the least of which was who would foot the bill for construction. This was the period when taxpayers were rebelling against pro teams that wanted them to pay for a palatial stadium many of them would never be able to set foot in.

Eventually, the numbers were hammered out. The Eagles would pay $330 million toward the project (and would also own the stadium, a first for the franchise), and the city of Philadelphia would contribute $95 million for land acquisition and site clearance. The state would also kick in $85 million, and Lincoln Financial Group would pay the Eagles nearly $6 million a year for the next 21 years for exclusive stadium-naming rights.

With the financing figured out, plans moved quickly from there and, in May 2001, construction began on the new 68,000-seat stadium that would include every modern amenity. There would be state-of-the-art luxury suites (double the amount at the Vet) and more than 3,000 luxury seats. For the average fan, there would be far more parking, wider seats, wider concourses, better scoreboards, and more—a lot more—restrooms. "Finally, finally, it's happened," quarterback Donovan McNabb said.

The Linc's first event, a soccer match, was held in August 2003, and the Eagles had a shakedown preseason game later in the month. The inaugural game was an emotional, raucous sight that included an appearance from Sylvester Stallone and prime time on *Monday Night Football* against the Tampa Bay Buccaneers.

And though the Eagles lost their first-ever home game in the Linc, the franchise had what it needed: a stadium to compete for the long term.

It was about time.

54 Norman Braman

In many respects, you have to be a little crazy and a little arrogant—on top of being all kinds of rich—to own a major sports franchise. That's obviously the case today, but even back in the old days, those were the requirements.

The Philadelphia Eagles have had their share of eccentric owners dating back to the beginning when Bert Bell decided it would be a great idea to bring pro football to Philly. So when Norman Braman bought the Eagles from the financially ruined Leonard Tose in 1985, it probably should have served as a cautionary tale for the guy who decided owning a pro football team was, in his words, "The ultimate fulfillment of every red-blooded American boy's fantasy."

Of course, he forgot to add that the price tag was a hefty $65 million, limiting that fantasy to just that—fantasy—for most red-blooded American boys.

But what Braman found was that wanting to own a team and actually doing it were two very different animals. On the one hand, he was one of America's richest men, owning a string of luxury car dealerships in Florida as well a world-class collection of modern art and a 4,000-bottle collection of the world's finest wines. On the other, he was renowned in his years owning the team as one of the game's true skinflints—and fans watched, horrified, as some of the best players in franchise history left for greener pastures.

Braman was another great example of a Philly kid who did well. He grew up in the Cobbs Creek section of Philadelphia and was a huge Eagles fans. He was a water boy at Eagles training camp in West Chester and often snuck into Shibe Park to watch them play. He graduated from Temple University and earned his fortune first in pharmaceuticals, then owned a string of drugstores before he began purchasing car dealerships.

Owning the Eagles was different from owning Cadillacs, but you'd be hard-pressed to convince Braman of that. Told once he was accused of running the Eagles franchise like a business, Braman just smiled. "I'll plead guilty to that," he said.

But while the team made money (nearly $50 million from 1985 to 1990), it came at a cost on the field. Braman was a hard-line opponent of free agency, and it was never more obvious than in 1993 when he let the team's best player, Reggie White, walk away without even making him an offer.

He also raised ticket prices three times in five seasons, cut back the college scouting department, and was renowned for underpaying his coaches. Soon Braman had the nickname, "Bottom Line Braman."

But he was ready to deal with it all if it meant success on the field. Unhappy with what he saw his first season, he fired coach Marion Campbell with just one game remaining in the 1985 season. After a lengthy search, Braman settled on the hiring of Buddy Ryan as the new coach. He liked Ryan's bravado and the job he had done with the Chicago Bears' Super Bowl–winning defense.

But what he liked from afar proved to be a disaster when they worked together. The two men simply could not stand each other. Braman wanted the respect he felt he deserved as Ryan's employer and the owner of the team. Ryan was from the old school and thought respect had to be earned and, to his mind, Braman had not earned it. Instead, Ryan often took shots at his owner, making fun of Braman's frequent trips to one of his homes in France. To Ryan, Braman was "the guy in France."

But Ryan also won football games, taking the Eagles to the playoffs three straight years.

Eventually Ryan's antics—and his inability to get out of the first round of the playoffs—gave Braman the excuse he needed to fire the coach, who didn't leave town quietly. "That guy has no idea what he's doing," Ryan said.

By 1994 Braman decided the fun of owning an NFL franchise was gone. With a revelation that he was paying himself a $7.5 million salary, Eagles fans had seen enough of him too. Sensing there was no better time than the present, he sold the Eagles to another guy who thought this was a dream come true—Jeffrey Lurie. The price tag? A reported $198 million, a record amount at that time for a professional sports franchise.

Braman settled back in Florida, where he continues to run his car dealerships in the Miami area, and is a financial supporter of numerous Republican candidates.

55 Jon Gruden

He coached with the Eagles for just three seasons, but Jon Gruden clearly, and perhaps permanently, left an impact. Consider the fact that after the 2010 season, the onetime Eagles offensive coordinator was the subject of more rumors than the fate of Jimmy Hoffa.

Gruden has one of the coaching résumés that make owners and general managers drool. He is the son of coach who worked his way up through the ranks the right way, learning the game from, just to name two, Bill Walsh and Mike Holmgren.

Indeed, Gruden got his first break in 1990 when the 49ers, and more specifically Holmgren, brought the 26-year-old in to be an "offensive quality-control coach," though few really knew what that meant.

In 1992, when Holmgren was hired as head coach of the Packers, he brought Gruden with him. The kid absorbed the West Coast offense like a sponge and, bit by bit, Holmgren gave him more responsibility. In 1993–94 Gruden took over as Green Bay's wide receivers coach, tutoring a young batch of receivers as well as handling the always prickly star Sterling Sharpe.

But Gruden got his biggest break to date the following year when Ray Rhodes, also an alumnus of the 49ers and Packers, took over as the Eagles' new head coach and immediately hired Gruden as his new offensive coordinator. Though it was the most responsibility he'd ever had as a coach, Gruden went in with supreme confidence because he knew he'd been trained by some of the best minds in the business.

He wasted no time installing the West Coast offense and convincing the players they could win with it. Incorporating recently acquired running back Ricky Watters and working with newly installed starting quarterback Rodney Peete, the Eagles finished 10–6. They reached the playoffs for the first time in four years and then hung up a club-playoff-record 58 points in a first-round win over the Detroit Lions.

The next season, Gruden was tested again when Peete went down with an injury and Ty Detmer took over as quarterback. Still, the Eagles went 10–6 again, finishing fourth in the NFC in total offense and getting back to the playoffs.

But the magic of the previous two seasons departed in 1997, mostly due to a spate of disastrous injuries on both sides of the ball. In addition, Gruden and Watters began to lock horns constantly, wrecking the team's fragile chemistry. Watters, who rushed for more than 1,000 yards in each of his three seasons in Philly, wanted the ball more. Gruden wanted him to play within the offense and take what was given. The conflicts and the injuries helped contribute to a 6–9–1 record.

But Gruden had shown more than enough to the rest of the league. His star was on the rise. In 1998 he was named head coach of the Oakland Raiders, a team he took to the playoffs in two of the four seasons he was there. In 2002 he was named head coach of the Tampa Bay Buccaneers and promptly took them to a Super Bowl victory.

After seven seasons in Tampa Bay, Gruden was fired and slipped into a role as color commentator on *Monday Night Football* along with Ron Jaworski, another Eagles alumnus.

For years afterward, and despite his professed happiness in the booth, Gruden has been the subject of numerous rumors involving several coaching positions.

And finally, in January 2018, Gruden did in fact return to the sidelines as head coach of the Raiders.

56 Merrill Reese

This is what it sounded like at the end of Super LII when the unthinkable became certain thanks to the voice that made everything real to Eagles fans.

"And the game is over! The Philadelphia Eagles are Super Bowl champions. For Eagles fans everywhere, this is for you. Let the celebration begin!"

You know that voice. No matter where you are and no matter what you're doing, you know that voice. Driving in the car or working in the yard or sitting on the deck, that voice is familiar, soothing, and identifiable. Merrill Reese and the Philadelphia Eagles—it seems there has never been one without the other.

Reese has been the play-by-play announcer for the Eagles Radio Network since 1977, and if it seems as if he's seen almost everything in the franchise's history, it's probably because he has.

He has watched the Eagles struggle and grow and thrive and struggle again. He has watched quarterbacks from Ron Jaworski to Randall Cunningham to Doug Pederson to Donovan McNabb and Michael Vick. He has seen coaches and owners come and go, and he has seen stadiums rise and fall. But his mellifluous baritone hasn't changed in all those years. Reese is now the longest-tenured play-by-play voice in the NFL and with the Super Bowl title at the end of the 2017 season, it has all been worthwhile—not that it ever wasn't.

"There's nothing else in the world I'd rather be doing," Reese has said more than once.

Fans know his every inflection, and there are contests every season to see which fan can imitate Reese the best. There's his trademark, "It's Goood," when the Eagles connect on a field goal. And there is the palpable love Reese clearly still has for the team.

He is Philadelphia born and bred and a graduate of Temple University, where, as an undergrad, he hosted a radio show with a Temple football player named Bill Cosby.

He got his break when he did some fill-in work at Philly's WIP and then helped out on Eagles preseason play-by-play when the regular voice, Charlie Swift, was on vacation.

In 1977 he took over as the Eagles' color analyst in tandem with Swift. But in December, the organization was rocked by the news that Swift committed suicide. Reese took over play-by-play duties, and former Packers star Herb Adderley took Reese's spot for the last two games of the season. Reese was given the job permanently and hasn't missed a game since.

Through the 2017 season, Reese has teamed with ex-Eagles wide receiver Mike Quick on the broadcasts, but over the years his color guys have also included Jim Barniak, Bill Bergey, and Stan Walters.

At age 75, Reese feels he is just reaching peak. "It never gets old," he said. "I'll never retire. They'll have to pry me out of the booth."

No, they won't, because for generations of fans, there are no Philadelphia Eagles without Merrill Reese.

57 Jerome Brown and Blenda Gay

They are the incidents that come from nowhere and shake the very foundation of credibility. They are the events that make you wonder why and how and force you to pause, reluctantly, and ask about what is important in life.

So it was in the stunning deaths of two Eagles—defensive tackle Jerome Brown and defensive end Blenda Gay. They came from different eras and, frankly, their circumstances could not have been more different.

Brown was as celebrated as Gay was obscure. Brown's loss, at the peak of his career, shook the Eagles to the core. Gay's death and the questions surrounding it left many puzzled and angry.

But in the end, two players from the Eagles family were dead, and they didn't have to be.

In 1992 Jerome Brown was just becoming the player everyone thought he could be. He was the Eagles' top draft pick and ninth overall in the 1987 draft. He'd been a controversial star at the University of Miami, but he had an uncanny ability to be in the right place at the right time and was developing into a first-class run-stopper in the NFL. Indeed, with ends Reggie White and Clyde Simmons and Brown in the middle, the Eagles had a defensive line for the ages.

The Eagles finished the 1991 season with a 10–6 record and were looking for big things in 1992, especially from Brown, who had lost 20 pounds and, in his own words, "matured." As it was, 1991 had been Brown's season, with 88 tackles and nine quarterback sacks, earning him his second-straight Pro Bowl berth.

But on June 25, 1992, Brown's Corvette skidded on wet pavement in his hometown of Brooksville, Florida, and crashed into a palm tree, killing Brown and his 12-year-old nephew, Gus. Jerome Brown was 27.

The loss shook the entire Eagles organization. In the Veterans Stadium locker room, they kept Brown's locker just the way it had been when he last used it, from where his shoes were stacked to where his helmet hung. In tribute, the players wore a *JB* patch on their jerseys that season. In the season opener, the Eagles also retired Brown's No. 99.

Perhaps the most dramatic gesture, though, came when the Eagles were preparing to play the New Orleans Saints in the play-offs in the Superdome. Unknown to the players, team managers brought Brown's gear to the game and set it up in a locker as though nothing had ever happened. It was a sign that Jerome was still with them. "It was definitely an inspiration," safety Wes Hopkins said. The Eagles took it from there, winning the game easily.

Blenda Gay's situation was different. He was a classic journeyman, battling just to get an opportunity to show what he could do. He'd played for tiny Fayetteville (North Carolina) State University and was a supplemental draft pick of the Oakland Raiders in 1973, where he was cut three times.

He played semipro ball before getting another shot with the San Diego Chargers in 1974. He was released after that season and signed by the Eagles. "He didn't have great talent, but he had great character," Eagles coach Dick Vermeil said.

Gay worked hard, stuck with the Eagles, and eventually turned himself into a solid defensive end. In 1976, as a starting end, he finished the season with 79 total tackles and two sacks.

On December 20, 1976, a week after the season had ended, the Eagles were shocked by news that Gay had been murdered by his wife Roxanne, who had slashed his throat with an eight-inch knife while Gay was asleep. Gay had been able to call for help but died on his way to the hospital. He was 26 years old.

From there, the stories diverge. Roxanne Gay claimed her 6'5", 255-pound husband had routinely assaulted her, and several friends corroborated her story. But others presented a story that she was a troubled, paranoid woman who routinely showed up at team practices to complain about the length of practices and to confront him about seeing other women. Psychiatrists and police found no evidence that Gay had assaulted his wife, and Roxanne Gay was charged with murder. She was found not guilty by reason of insanity. She was sent to the Trenton Psychiatric Hospital in New Jersey and was released in 1980.

"It's a tragic thing," Vermeil said after the incident. "Here's a young man with everything going for him, and now he's gone."

58 Ray Rhodes

There are some men who were born to be head coaches. There are some men who were born to be great assistant coaches but were cursed with the belief that they were destined for far more. Ray Rhodes fit into the latter category.

Brilliant, obsessed, profane, and puzzling, Rhodes cut his coaching teeth as a defensive coordinator with the San Francisco 49ers, then with the Green Bay Packers before returning to the 49ers. He had five Super Bowl rings in his years with the 49ers, and he believed, perhaps accurately at the time, that he was head-coaching caliber.

So did the Eagles, who hired him as head coach in 1995 to replace the disastrous Rick Kotite. In Rhodes, team owner Jeffrey Lurie saw a coach who could bring the discipline, drive, and ability necessary to turn the Eagles into a contender. And over the course of four turbulent seasons, Rhodes took the Eagles to the heights and back down again, nearly wrecking his health in the process. It was a meteoric rise and an equally rapid descent.

"I've been a part of five world championships," Rhodes said in his introductory press conference. "I've been there. It's not hearsay. I didn't come here to lose. Ray Rhodes is not about losing, man." And that attitude carried over to the field, where Rhodes led the overachieving Eagles to a 10–6 regular-season record and a spot in the playoffs, where they crushed the Detroit Lions 58–37 before being eliminated the next week by the Cowboys.

But the foundation appeared to be set for greatness. For his efforts, Rhodes was named the Associated Press NFL Coach of the Year, an impressive accomplishment for someone who had no head-coaching experience.

In 1996 the Eagles started off 7–2, including impressive road wins over division rivals Washington, New York, and Dallas. But Philadelphia dropped four of its last seven games and played listlessly in a 14–0 playoff loss to the 49ers.

In 1997 injuries decimated the Eagles, and they toppled to 6–9–1. But cracks in the foundation grew even larger when Rhodes began to question the toughness of his team and insinuate that the players were not together as a unit. That's a bad combination, especially in a team sport.

By 1998 a tenure that had begun with so much promise was collapsing at light speed. The moody, irascible Rhodes had all but given up, and the Eagles fell to a disastrous 3–13 record. Lurie had seen enough and, after four seasons, he fired Rhodes. Just a few days later, the Packers, who had just watched Mike Holmgren leave for Seattle, focused on Rhodes as the replacement.

Green Bay general manger Ron Wolf, convinced the Packers had grown soft and disinterested under Holmgren, wanted a head coach who would reignite the fire, and he was convinced Rhodes was that coach.

But after one season, the same issues resurfaced that had dogged Rhodes his final season in Philly. Players began to tune out Rhodes and his message. But unlike Philadelphia, where it took four years, the Packers stopped listening around midseason.

The Packers beat the Arizona Cardinals to close out the season with an 8–8 record. The strange thing was, if circumstances had worked out a little differently, the Packers would have reached the playoffs. Instead, they were left out, and Wolf, distressed at how far his team had fallen, fired Rhodes that night.

Since then, Rhodes has returned to what he knows best—defense—and has served as defensive coordinator for the Washington Redskins, Denver Broncos, and Seattle Seahawks and as an assistant with the Houston Texans and Cleveland Browns. He has never been a candidate for another head-coaching position.

59 Clyde Simmons

He could have been the greatest defensive lineman in Philadelphia Eagles history. The only problem was that he was already playing alonsgside the greatest defensive lineman in Philadelphia Eagles history.

Clyde Simmons was a 6'6", 280-pound whirling dervish of rage that, when he was wound up and ready to go, was practically unblockable.

At the height of his career, even White acknowledged how good his teammate was. "Clyde is on par with anybody in the league," White said. "He's come that far."

Simmons remains No. 2 in club history in quarterback sacks with 76½ and still holds the Eagles' official record for most sacks in a game with 4½, set against the Cowboys in 1991. But his greatness was overshadowed by the imposing visage of White, who took the game to another level. For his part, Simmons never complained about being overlooked. In fact, he preferred it. "I don't need to bother with that mess," he said. "I like my privacy."

He was in line to have all the privacy he wanted during the 1986 NFL Draft. Considered too small to play defensive end, along with the fact that he played at a small college (Western Carolina), NFL teams were not exactly lining up to draft him. But Eagles coach Buddy Ryan was intrigued by Simmons' speed and decided to draft him in the ninth round. After spending a season on special teams and learning how to play Ryan's way, Simmons slipped into a starting role in 1987. And he took off from there.

In his first two seasons as a bookend with White, Simmons posted 14 sacks, scored a touchdown, and added a safety. In 1989 Simmons had the kind of season most defensive ends can only imagine as he recorded 15½ sacks and even returned an interception for a touchdown. But he received little national notoriety, though was named the Eagles' defensive MVP.

"It's a shame," said Eagles defensive coordinator Bud Carson. "Clyde should be an All-Pro, but he's a victim of playing on the same line with Reggie White."

By 1991, despite a testy training-camp holdout, Simmons could not be ignored any longer. He added 13 sacks and earned his first All-Pro acknowledgement, and in 1992 he was even better, posting an NFL-best 19 sacks, just two off the all-time record set by White five years earlier.

In 1993 Simmons' mentor and friend, White, left via free agency, and he stayed only one more season before signing his own free-agent deal with the Arizona Cardinals in 1994. He would also play for the Jacksonville Jaguars, Cincinnati Bengals, and Chicago Bears before retiring after the 2000 season. Simmons finished his career with 121½ quarterback sacks, 14th-best in NFL history.

In 2010, after working briefly for a mortgage company and probation officer, Simmons returned to what he knew best—football. He was hired by the New York Jets as a fellowship coach and, two years later, took over as assistant defensive line coach for the St. Louis (and then Los Angeles) Rams. In 2017, he was named defensive line coach for the Cleveland Browns.

60 Trent Cole

Eagles defensive end Trent Cole spent seven seasons patrolling the defense and terrorizing opposing quarterbacks in ways unseen since the halcyon days of Reggie White and Clyde Simmons. Indeed, had he stayed healthy, he could have challenged team sack numbers no one thought were assailable.

But it was not to be.

The Eagles were intrigued by Cole, a star at the University of Cincinnati, in the 2005 NFL Draft because he never seemed to let up from first play to last. Draft pundits like to call it a great "motor," but the Eagles just liked the fact he never quit. So they made him a fifth-round pick, and he did not disappoint. "I can't get him out of the game," Reid said during Cole's first season, when he posted five sacks in 15 games. "He's relentless."

He added eight more in 2006, and the Eagles knew they had something special, so they renegotiated his contract and signed him through the 2013 season. All Cole did in 2007 was respond with his best season to date, recording 103 total tackles and a team-high 12½ sacks to earn his Pro Bowl berth. Two years later, after another 12½ sacks, he was named to his second Pro Bowl.

An avid hunter, Cole has become a fan favorite because of his enthusiastic celebratory dances after sacks and because of that "motor," which never seems to be idle. "That's the only way I know how to play," Cole said. "I know if there's a way I can get to the quarterback, I'm going to find a way to do it. I don't care what it takes."

After the 2014 season, the Eagles released Cole, whose 85½ sacks was second in team history behind White. A week later he signed with the Indianapolis Colts, but it wasn't the same. Injuries and time had robbed him of his explosiveness and after a subpar 2015 and '16 season, he was released. In December 2017, Cole officially retired as an Eagle.

61 Mike Mamula

Mike Mamula is on the list whether he deserves to be or not. Eagles fans know exactly what list that is too. The one titled *Greatest Draft Mistakes of All Time.* The former Boston College defensive end is on that list with Tony Mandarich and JaMarcus Russell and Ryan Leaf and Steve Emtman and David Klingler and so many others. Fair? Maybe not, but perception is reality, especially in the NFL.

Mamula has gone down in Eagles history as a player who did not excel to his lofty draft status. But whose fault was that?

In 1994 Mamula was one of the dominant defensive ends in college football, recording 17 sacks despite playing as an undersized 250-pounder. Nonetheless, despite having a year of college eligibility left, Mamula decided to take his chance in the NFL Draft. To many general managers and scouts, he was, in the vernacular, "just a guy." He was nothing special. He was too small, too slow, too… everything. He tried hard and was tough, but at the very best he was a third-round pick, and then he'd likely have to be moved to linebacker. At least that was the consensus.

But that was before Mamula's stunning performance in the February 1995 NFL Combine, a place where college talent can show their stuff to eagle-eyed teams. In the months leading up to the combine, Mamula trained with BC strength-and-conditioning coach Jerry Palmieri, who stressed practicing the same skills over and over that would be required at the NFL Combine.

"I went to the Combine having done every test hundreds of times, while some other guys had never done some of the specific drills," Mamula told ESPN several years ago. As a result, Mamula's 40-yard dash time (a staple of the Combine) was faster than some linebackers, and his strength rivaled some offensive lineman. Strength and speed, what else could an NFL general manager want?

What followed was a little misdirection, a little miscalculation, and a lot of second-guessing. As the draft approached, word was leaked that the Tampa Bay Buccaneers, which had the seventh pick overall, were enamored of Mamula and would take him at that spot. But the Eagles, who had the 12th selection, liked him a lot too—perhaps too much.

On draft day, the Eagles offered their pick and two second-round selections to the Bucs for their seventh pick. The Bucs jumped at it. Now at No. 7, the Eagles quickly selected Mamula, a guy they were convinced would redefine the defensive-end position and would make Eagles fans forget the departed Reggie White.

The Buccaneers? They later admitted they had no interest in Mamula and used the No. 12 pick for Warren Sapp. They also did some more maneuvering and selected linebacker Derrick Brooks later in the first round. Sapp anchored Tampa Bay's defensive line for nearly a decade, and Brooks evolved into one the game's best linebackers and, with those two leading the way, the Bucs eventually won a Super Bowl.

Mamula's career did not unfold as anyone had hoped. Burdened with the unreasonable expectations that came with being an elite draft pick, Mamula quickly clashed with Philly's tough media. Fans expected him to dominate, but he did not and could not, especially when he was giving up nearly 100 pounds to some offensive tackles.

He played five seasons for the Eagles before injuries ended his career. He had his best season in 1999, when he recorded 8½ sacks. He finished his career with 31½ sacks. Those aren't bad numbers, but they are hardly what fans expected from a top-flight pick.

The First Pick

Bert Bell's great idea would finally get some practical application in 1936. His Eagles had been the worst team in the NFL in 1935, posting a dismal 2–9 record and leading Bell to fire his good friend Lud Wray as head coach.

In his place stepped Bell himself, and his plan was simple: he would use the new NFL Draft, an idea he sold the rest of the NFL on, to improve the Eagles. So in February 1936 Bell set his sights on the reigning Heisman Trophy winner, University of Chicago running back Jay Berwanger. His selection would infuse the Eagles with the talent they needed, even the league playing field, and spark interest in a fan base that was not yet convinced of the new franchise.

There was only one problem for Bell and, yes, it was a big one: Berwanger didn't want to play in the NFL. With a business degree from the prestigious University of Chicago, Berwanger wanted to instead go into business, where he could make some real money. Bell tried to change Berwanger's mind, and eventually Chicago Bears coach George Halas purchased Berwanger's rights from Bell for $16,000. But even Halas couldn't change the running back's mind, and when Berwanger said he would sign a two-year no-cut contract for $25,000, even Halas walked away. Berwanger never did play football and instead became a multimillionaire in the rubber and plastic industry.

Philly's second-round pick that year, John McCauley, never played either, nor did their first-round pick the next year, Sam Francis, a back from Nebraska.

Finally, in 1938, the Eagles selected Ohio State's Jim McDonald with their first pick, and he never played for them, later spending two years with Detroit. The first top-notch Eagles first-round pick didn't come until 1939 when they drafted TCU quarterback Davey O'Brien.

To Bell's credit, though, the NFL Draft has become the lifeblood of the league.

Mamula still resides in the Philadelphia area with his family and started a drug screening and background check company called Comprehensive Screening Solutions.

Was he a bust? Some say yes, some say no. Should the Eagles have selected him so high? Hindsight is 20/20.

For his part, Mamula has no regrets. "I played hard, and I enjoyed my time there," he said.

62 Ricky Watters

There may have been worse ways for Ricky Watters to start his career with the Philadelphia Eagles—but not many. He could have expressed his love for Tom Landry or declared the Liberty Bell overrated or even professed his distaste for cheesesteaks and the newest Eagles running back would not have enraged fans as much as he did after his first game on September 3, 1995.

Watters came to the Eagles as a high-profile free agent from the San Francisco 49ers and as part of new coach Ray Rhodes' rebuilding effort. He was going to provide a spark, a presence, and the offense the team had lacked.

But, in a postgame incident that has taken on mythical qualities, Watters left the kind of impression a new employee, especially one who has just signed a three-year, $6.9 million contract, really doesn't want to leave.

Watters had played badly anyway, losing two fumbles in the Eagles' 21–6 loss to Tampa Bay. But he also failed to extend his hands to catch two passes that were imminently catchable, so he was asked by the media afterward about his case of alligator arms.

His response still rankles Eagles fans. "For who? For what?" Watters replied, suggesting he wasn't going to get hurt trying to catch a stupid pass. It suggested selfishness and a self-centered nature, and those four words created a whirlwind of criticism. And few can criticize the way Eagles fans and the Philadelphia media can.

Perhaps overwhelmed by the reaction or perhaps understanding just how badly he sounded when he said it, Watters called a press conference two days later and asked for forgiveness. He apologized to everyone he could think of and said his comments were totally out of character for him. In truth, his history suggested they probably weren't, but Watters' emotional mea culpa seemed to calm the waters, so to speak, and he went on to produce three excellent seasons for the Eagles.

He began his career with the 49ers, playing three seasons there and capping them with three touchdowns in a rout of the San Diego Chargers in Super Bowl XXIX. He then joined the Eagles and, after his rocky start, produced in a way few players for the franchise have before or since.

He led the league with 1,855 total yards in 1996, including 1,411 on the ground (still second-best in team history) and helped get the Eagles into the playoffs. In his three seasons, he led the team in rushing, piling up a total of 3,794 yards, still sixth-best in team history, while scoring 31 touchdowns. He was named All-Pro in both 1995 and 1996 and was a Pro Bowler both years, so no one could accurately say he wasn't worth the cost—at least on the field.

But the issue that poked its head up in that first game in 1995 eventually led to Watters' desire, and need, to move on again. He clashed with another strong personality, offensive coordinator Jon Gruden, about Watters' role in the offense. It was an argument Watters wasn't going to win. Still, Gruden tried to downplay any controversy. "There are a lot of negative clouds around Ricky sometimes because of his emotions," Gruden said. "But he certainly backs it up on Sunday. When he's on the field, he doesn't think anybody can tackle him. He's beautiful that way." In other ways? Not so much.

Watters admitted his emotions would often get the better of him and he'd storm off the field or argue with teammates.

Finally, after the 1997 season, the Eagles decided it was best for everyone if he moved on, and Watters was not offered a new contract. He signed with the Seattle Seahawks and played four more seasons.

He is now a motivational speaker and is in the music industry as a recording artist and producer. And he wrote a book that, to the surprise of no one, is titled *For Who, For What? A Warrior's Journey*. He also returned to his alma mater, Notre Dame, in 2014 and earned his graphic design degree.

63 Cris Carter

In the end, the three turbulent years Cris Carter spent with the Philadelphia Eagles and the way he departed were probably the best things that ever happened to him.

There were the battles with his coaches, the war with coach Buddy Ryan, the drugs and the alcohol, the rumors of a guy who was so talented and so lazy and, finally, the embarrassment of being released at the prime of his career. In the end, all that helped make Cris Carter the player he ended up being. But it was a long, painful journey.

Carter should have been a star in Philly. He should have had Eagles fans eating out of the palm of his hand. He was that talented and that explosive, but a bad attitude fueled by an insatiable need for drugs and alcohol destroyed that. It was only after he left the Eagles and learned what it was like to work hard and commit to being the best that he became the player who is now on the verge of being inducted into the Pro Football Hall of Fame.

Carter was a star athlete in high school and one of the top wide receivers in the country at Ohio State. But even there, the seeds of trouble were already sown. Prior to his senior season, he secretly signed with an agent, a violation of NCAA rules. That infraction resulted in Carter being suspended for the entire 1987 college season. Later that year, he was taken by the Eagles in the fourth round of the NFL supplemental draft, and Buddy Ryan couldn't wait to get his hands on him. "All he does," Ryan said famously, "is score touchdowns."

But he did more than that. He alienated teammates with a selfish attitude, and he alienated the Philly media with his standoff-ishness—and annoying the Philly media is never a good idea. But Ryan was right about one thing: he knew how to score touchdowns.

Indeed, in his first season, he caught just five passes but two went for touchdowns, including his first pro catch against the Cardinals.

In 1988 he caught 39 passes and tied for the team lead with six touchdowns, and the following season, he caught 45 more passes, 11 for touchdowns, which was third-best in the NFC. But by that stage, Carter was spiraling downward from his addictions.

"Cris has always been all or nothing," Keith Byars, a teammate of Carter's at both Ohio State and with the Eagles, told *Sports Illustrated* a few years ago. "That's good when it's channeled in the right direction. But when he was doing the wrong things, he was committed to that, too. When he was doing drugs and alcohol, I'm sure he was trying to be the best addict out there."

The Eagles, and especially Ryan, saw what was happening and decided they needed to cut their losses. In a stunning surprise to everyone, the Eagles released Carter in the 1990 preseason. Today, Carter credits Ryan's decision with helping him and, in fact, considers being cut as a favor.

Carter was claimed by the Minnesota Vikings just before the start of the 1990 season and, given another chance, he flourished. Over the next 12 seasons with the Vikings, Carter was a Pro Bowler eight straight seasons (1993–2000), a two-time All-Pro, a member of the NFL's All-Decade Team for the 1990s, and NFL Man of the Year. He finished his career with 1,101 receptions, third-best in NFL history, and just missed being inducted into the Pro Football Hall of Fame in 2011.

A football analyst with Fox Sports after a long stint at ESPN, Carter continues to thank the Eagles for what they did so many years ago. "I tell people now when they see alcoholics and drug addicts on the street, they should think of me," said Carter, who says he hasn't had a drink or touched drugs since 1990. "I'm lucky."

And, after six years of waiting, in February 2013 Carter was finally inducted into the Pro Football Hall of Fame.

64 Frank "Bucko" Kilroy

Depending on whom you were talking to at the time, Frank "Bucko" Kilroy was either the toughest player in the NFL or the dirtiest. Maybe he was both. "I was just a heavy hitter," Kilroy said later. "We were hard people back then, and some guys were just naturally heavy hitters. It was a different time."

It was the NFL of the late 1940s and early 1950s, when players routinely played both offense and defense for next to no money and rarely, if ever, complained. It was not a game for the faint-hearted, and it was certainly not a game for those who didn't know what they were getting themselves into.

Kilroy was tailor-made for that era. He was rough and tough and rugged and looked, according to one writer at the time, "like an unmade bed." And Kilroy reveled in all of it.

He did not play football in high school or college and, after graduating from Philly's Temple University, went into the merchant marines during World War II. During a break with the merchant marines, he tried out for the Steagles and earned a spot on the team. He ended up playing 13 NFL season, all with the Eagles, and was named All-Pro three times as an offensive guard (1947–49) and three other times as a defensive middle guard (1952–54). He was also a critical member of the Eagles' two NFL championship teams in 1948 and 1949.

The Suicide Seven

It seemed like a good idea at the time. Even in the 1950s teams were seeking new and better ways to draw attention to what they were doing, and Eagles publicity director Ed Hogan came up with a beauty.

In an effort to publicize the Eagles rugged and talented defense of the early 1950s, Hogan came up with the nickname "the Suicide Seven." The players included Norm "Wildman" Willey, Mike Jarmoluk, Frank "Bucko" Kilroy, Chuck Bednarik, Wayne Robinson, Jess Richardson, and Tom Scott.

And to drive home the image even more, Hogan set up a photo with the seven sitting in their helmets and shoulder pads, wearing eye patches and holding pistols in the style of pirates. They were posed at a poker table, looking properly fearsome, pointing their pistols at tight end Bobby Walston, who was dealing the cards.

Of course, there wasn't mass media like there is today, and no one really knows how popular the photo was or how many fans actually saw it.

Fortunately, the name Suicide Seven didn't last long either, though the Eagles' defense was considered one of the dirtiest in the league at the time.

But as good a player as he was, his reputation was built on the fact that many opponents saw him, simply, as a dirty player. One opponent, New York Giants lineman Al DeRogatis, accused Kilroy of biting his nose. Kilroy denied it. "I bit his ear," he said.

Perhaps Kilroy is best known as a defendant in a libel trial against *Life* magazine, which in 1955 ran an article titled "Savagery on Sunday," describing in graphic photos and words the violence of pro football. And Kilroy was a central figure in the story. Furious at how he was portrayed ("the toughest of the bad men"), he took the magazine to court seeking $250,000 in damages. He was joined by teammate Wayne Robinson, who was also singled out in the piece.

Kilroy defended his play and his personality, going so far as to say that as a kid he'd been a choirboy at St. Anne's Roman Catholic Church in Port Richmond, Pennsylvania. It also didn't hurt that the trial, which didn't take place until two years after the story appeared, took place in his hometown of Philadelphia.

In the end, the jury found in favor of Kilroy and Robinson but only awarded them $11,600 each. But as both men pointed out, that award was still far more than they made playing for the Eagles.

Kilroy finished his career in 1955 as a player/coach for the Eagles and then went into a long, successful career in player development. From 1956 to 1970 he worked in personnel and scouting for the Eagles, Redskins, and Cowboys. In 1971 he joined the New England Patriots as their player-personnel director and helped build the Patriots into a solid, respectable franchise. He is also credited with creating the National Football Scouting Combine and has been called one of the greatest personnel evaluators in NFL history.

In July 2007 Kilroy died at age 86 and was buried in Norwood, Massachusetts.

65 Tim Rossovich

Oh, those stories. There was glass eating (never proven) and the spider eating (which was). He would enliven parties by setting himself on fire. (Though he had a secret: "Wear two shirts," he said. "The first one burns, but the second doesn't.") He would uncork Gregorian chants in the middle of team meetings and jump out of the bushes and terrify teammates walking in the door. And, of course, there was the wild hair and mustache that looked as though it had taken on a life of its own.

Tim Rossovich was an honest-to-God counterculture maniac, born and bred in California in the teeth of the rebellious 1960s. And for four years, he entertained, enthralled, and infuriated everyone he came in contact with as a member of the Philadelphia Eagles.

But what many people forget is that Rossovich could play. An All-American at the University of Southern California, he captained the Trojans' 1967 national championship team and was the Eagles' top draft pick in 1968.

"I had no expectations," Rossovich said once. "I wanted to play baseball." Indeed, he was such a good athlete, he was drafted by the Pittsburgh Pirates out of high school. But deciding he didn't want to deal with the rigors of the minor leagues, he decided to play football for USC and then took his talents and outsized personality to the Eagles.

As might be expected, it wasn't a great fit, especially since he ended up playing for three coaches in a matter of four seasons—and each tolerated Rossovich's antics less than the last. In addition, in Rossovich's four seasons from 1968 to 1971, the Eagles put some

Eagles linebacker Tim Rossovich in 1970. Rossovich caused mild controversy on the Eagles because of his sometimes bizarre behavior...and because of his hair.

of their worst teams ever on the field. Had they been contenders, he may well have been one of the NFL's great characters.

In 1969 Rossovich earned All-Pro honors at defensive end, but in 1970, new coach Jerry Williams had a hole at middle linebacker with the premature retirement of Dave Lloyd. Williams asked Rossovich if he would take over as middle linebacker, a position he had never played before. "Jerry said he thought the best athlete should play middle linebacker, and he wanted me to do it," Rossovich said. "I said sure."

Rossovich proceeded to learn all he could about the position by studying hour after hour of film of the game's best linebacker at the time—the Chicago Bears' Dick Butkus. The result was that Rossovich made himself into a solid, reliable middle linebacker.

But while he took his performance on the field seriously, he never lost his individualism. In 1971 another new coach, Ed Khayat, ordered all his players to shave their mustaches and cut their hair. Not surprisingly, Rossovich rebelled. "[Khayat] says it will help discipline," Rossovich groused. "It will hurt discipline. Instead of talking about football, we're talking about mustaches and sideburns." He eventually complied with the edict and played well, but he would never forget how ridiculous the policy was.

The following season, Rossovich refused to report to training camp as part of a contract dispute. Fed up, general manager Pete Retzlaff took the option available to many teams then—he traded Rossovich to the San Diego Chargers for a first-round draft pick in 1973.

And so it was over. Rossovich played two seasons with the Chargers, hooked on to the ill-fated World Football League, and then tried one more time in the NFL before calling it quits and going into an acting career.

He now lives in California and works with his wife in a rescue foundation for dogs.

He swears he no longer eats glass.

66 Roman Gabriel

In some ways, the 1972 season was the worst in Eagles history. Sure there were seasons during which they had won fewer games, but for sheer ineptitude, the '72 campaign under head coach Ed Khayat probably took the cake.

In the end the Eagles posted a 2–11–1 record, beating only the Houston Oilers and Kansas City Chiefs (both by one point) and tying the St. Louis Cardinals. But what made the season particularly painful was that in 14 games, the Eagles scored just 12 touchdowns—all season.

Certainly it didn't help that season that the Eagles were ripped apart by serious injuries to some key offensive talent. But still…12 touchdowns?

The single-biggest reason for the offensive disaster was actually pretty simple—the Eagles had no one to play quarterback. After trading Norm Snead in 1971, the Eagles went with Pete Liske under center, and he was something less than awe-inspiring. In 1972 the Eagles decided to start their first-round draft pick, John Reaves. He was even worse.

So as the 1973 season loomed, team owner Leonard Tose, embarrassed and angry by what he'd seen on the field, decided enough was enough. He decided to make a play for an established NFL quarterback who could work with the young talent he was convinced was already in place.

That January Tose and Mike McCormack, who had just replaced Khayat as head coach, flew to California to meet with Los Angeles Rams owner Carroll Rosenbloom in an effort to swing a deal—a big deal—that would bring former league MVP Roman Gabriel to Philly.

For Gabriel, who had spent the previous 11 seasons with the Rams, the deal sounded like a good idea. A North Carolina native, he was looking to get back East to be closer to family anyway, and he knew the Rams were ready to move on without him.

The negotiations weren't easy, especially since Rosenbloom kept changing the terms of the deal. But finally, in June, the two sides agreed and Gabriel—the established, veteran quarterback the Eagles desperately needed—was on his way to Philadelphia.

But he didn't come cheap. In exchange for Gabriel, the Eagles had to send the Rams wide receiver Harold Jackson, running back Tony Baker, a first-round draft pick in 1974, and a first- and third-round pick in 1975.

"Mike said that with my experience and leadership, he felt with a young football team that I'd feel like Moses," Gabriel said years later. And Gabriel wasted no time demonstrating those leadership skills McCormack was convinced his new team needed. In his introductory press conference in Philadelphia, Gabriel boldly proclaimed, "I feel that in two years, we'll have a world championship in Philadelphia."

Obviously that didn't transpire, but Gabriel still infused the young team with a toughness and work ethic it had lacked. In his first season with the Eagles, he led the league in completions (270), pass attempts (460), yards (3,219), and touchdown passes (23). Remember, in the season before the Eagles had scored just 12. And though the Eagles were still only 5–8–1 in 1973, one of those victories came against the powerful Dallas Cowboys. Gabriel was named NFL Comeback Player of the Year and was hailed as the messiah by the Eagles' long-suffering fans. "The trade for Gabe made us a football team," McCormack said.

But the momentum ground to a halt the next season when the NFL Players Association went on strike prior to training camp. Gabriel initially sided with the union and stayed away. But citing loyalty to Tose and to an organization that had helped resurrect his career, he crossed the picket line and went into camp. That move infuriated the veteran players, and he was never really trusted again.

Gabriel struggled that season and was benched the final three games in favor of rookie Mike Boryla. In 1975 Gabriel was back as starter, but a 2–8 start sent him back to the bench in favor of Boryla.

In 1976 McCormack was fired, and Dick Vermeil, with whom Gabriel had worked in L.A. when Vermeil was the Rams' special-teams coach, took over. Vermeil had other ideas about what he wanted to do at quarterback, and Gabriel, who was trying to recover from a serious knee injury, was told it might be time for him to retire. But Gabriel wasn't ready to quit just yet.

Then with six weeks left in the season, Eagles offensive coordinator John Idzik called Gabriel, who was working out on his own in California. He asked him to come back and try playing because, "You're better with one knee than the kid we have now with two."

He started the final four games of a 4–10 season and, having proven what he needed to prove, retired after the 1977 season.

He was not the player in Philly he had been for so many years with the Rams, but he still brought an attitude the franchise needed. And three years later, the Eagles fulfilled Gabriel's promise of a few years earlier by winning the NFC title and getting to their first Super Bowl.

Gabriel went on to do a little acting and a little coaching, but now he lives in Charlotte, North Carolina, and works on various charitable foundations.

67 Bill Bradley

There really wasn't much Bill Bradley couldn't do. Despite his size—a mere 5'11" and 190 pounds—he was a star quarterback first in high school and then at the University of Texas. He was a talented receiver and a terrific punter. And, for good measure, he could play a little bit in the defensive backfield. And he could talk. Oh my, could he talk—to anyone, anywhere, and at any time. He could talk the frosting off a cake and come back for more.

Bill Bradley was another one of those players from the late 1960s who didn't just march to the beat of his own drummer—he marched to his own marching band. Good natured and irreverent, he grew up in Palestine, Texas, where he was such a great athlete growing up, he was dubbed "Super Bill."

In 1969 he was the third-round draft pick of the Eagles and, like so many young players, did his penance sitting on the sideline watching the veterans.

Unfortunately for Bradley, the Eagles were horrendous in those days. In his first season, Philly finished 4–9–1, and in one particularly awful performance, the Eagles were being thrashed by the Dallas Cowboys. Bradley figured that was as good a time as any for him to get some experience.

Let Bradley take it from here: "In the middle of the third quarter, it was way out of hand, so I walked up to [defensive coordinator] Jimmy Carr and said 'Hey Coach, why don't you let some of us rookies play? Because of the fact that you won't get the veterans hurt, and it will give you a chance to look at some of the rookies. This game's over with.'"

Carr ignored the upstart kid for a while until he came back and pleaded his case—again and again.

"Finally in the middle of the fourth quarter, I did it again, and Jimmy said, 'OK, Bradley, just get the hell in there.'" And with that, a little Eagles history was made and Eagles fans got their first look at a player who would become one of their favorites for years.

Lined up at free safety, Bradley saw the Cowboys quarterback focus on tight end Mike Ditka. Bradley jumped the route, intercepted the pass, and returned it 56 yards for the touchdown. It was his first time ever touching a football in the NFL, and he had scored a touchdown.

But so confident, so brash, was this kid that 10 yards from the goal line he held the ball up in triumph, despite the fact that the Eagles were losing by almost 30 points. The move so enraged Cowboys wide receiver Bob Hayes, who was chasing the rookie, that once Bradley reached the end zone, Hayes clobbered him, earning a personal-foul penalty.

It was just the start for Bradley, who truly became one of the most popular players in team history. As one of his teammates once said, "[Eagles fans] boo everybody from Santa Claus to Ronald McDonald to a squirrel running cross the field. But they never did boo Bill Bradley."

In eight seasons with the Eagles, he was selected to three Pro Bowls, and his 34 career interceptions are tied for the team lead with Eric Allen and Brian Dawkins.

In 1972 Bradley led the NFL with a career-best 11 interceptions (in a 14-game season) and followed that up with nine more interceptions in 1973, the first player in the NFL history to lead the league in interceptions two straight seasons. "The interceptions came from studying, I think," Bradley said years later. "Playing quarterback in college helped me a little, but it was mostly anticipation and knowing where the quarterback was going."

One thing he didn't anticipate was the lack of patience the Eagles front office had with contract disputes. Both Bradley and teammate Tim Rossovich decided to stay away from training camp in 1972 to protest their salaries. In response, the Eagles traded Rossovich, and Bradley had second thoughts and reported to camp.

Not surprisingly, after he retired, the cerebral Bradley went into coaching. He has coached in college, the USFL, the CFL, and the NFL. In 2014, he retired from coaching and lives in Texas.

68 Joe Kuharich

There wasn't middle ground on the topic of one Joseph Lawrence Kuharich. He was either completely misunderstood, a victim of bad luck and maybe runaway hubris, or, as many Eagles fans still believe, the worst coach in team history.

Too dramatic a statement? Hardly. After all, in the minds of many fans, he was the guy solely responsible for dealing away the very foundation and heart of a franchise that, only four years earlier, had won an NFL title.

With dizzying speed, he got rid of his best quarterback, Sonny Jurgensen; wide receiver Tommy McDonald; linebacker Lee Roy Caffey; and several others. In return he got next to nothing. And when fans complained, Kuharich ignored them, convinced he would prove everyone wrong. He didn't.

"To play for this team, a player must show he wants to be part of the organization," he once said. But instead of building a strong team pulling in one direction, his teams were, frankly, a mess. In five seasons, the Eagles had just one winning season and even then did not reach the playoffs.

Kuharich, who had solid credentials, nonetheless wasn't an especially popular choice when he was hired by owner Jerry

The Three-Headed Monster

In 1966 Joe Kuharich was faced with a problem—well, three problems. He had three quarterbacks on the roster he liked but not enough to hand the starting job to any one of them. There was Norm Snead, who came to the Eagles as part of the controversial Sonny Jurgensen trade two years earlier; there was King Hill, who had been with the team since 1961; and there was Jack Concannon, a second-round draft pick in 1964.

None of the three could take command of the position singlehandedly, so Kuharich devised an unusual solution. That season, he played a game of musical quarterbacks, driving the players and fans crazy.

"It became a joke around the league," Hill said later. "But the three of us weren't laughing. I thought Joe was a nice fellow, but I can't say I understood him too well."

Amazingly, the system worked pretty well, as the Eagles ran off seven wins in their final nine games, posted a 9–5 record, and finished second in the division. It was also Kuharich's only winning season in his five as Philly's head coach.

What angered the three quarterbacks so much, though, was their belief that Kuharich was playing each one against the others in hopes of getting a better performance. He would tell one quarterback in practice that he would be starting the next game, but he would also tell the other two the same thing.

For the season, Snead completed just 46 percent of his passes with eight touchdowns and 11 interceptions (and he was the team leader). Hill completed 55 percent of his passes, but he threw seven interceptions and just five touchdown passes while Concannon brought up the rear, completing just 21 of 51 passes. The combined quarterback efficiency rating was a pallid 53.4, one of the worst in team history.

The experiment lasted just a year. By the start of the 1967 season, Concannon had been traded, and the offense belonged to Snead, who proceeded to throw for more than 3,300 yards and 29 touchdowns.

Wolman, given the title of head coach and general manager, and told to do what needed to be done. The results were another painful era in Eagles history, damaging Kuharich's legacy, which had started strongly with successful stints at the University of San Francisco and in six seasons as head coach of the Washington Redskins.

But his career in Philadelphia never got off the ground. In fact, in what proved to be his last season as head coach, in 1968, Kuharich had to deal with the full wrath of truly angry Eagles fans. It didn't help that Philly lost its first 11 games that season. At every home game, the chant of "Joe must go!" would reverberate around Franklin Field. Rumors swirled that Kuharich's life was in danger, forcing plainclothes policemen to accompany the coach everywhere he went.

Prior to the final home game, a group of ticket holders called the Committee to Rejuvenate the Philadelphia Eagles tried to organize a movement that would convince season-ticket holders to boycott the final game as a protest. The Eagles won the game but lost out on the opportunity to gain the top pick in the next draft—who ended up being a running back named O.J. Simpson.

In five seasons Kuharich managed just a 28–41–1 record and left the franchise in just about the lowest ebb it had ever been in. In May 1969 Wolman sold the team to Leonard Tose, and Kuharich was fired. He slipped away from football after that but did come back to the Eagles under Dick Vermeil as a part-time scout.

But Kuharich was being ravaged by cancer and, on January 25, 1981—the day the Eagles played in their first Super Bowl—Kuharich died.

69 Bill Bergey

He seemed to be everywhere. The familiar No. 66, with the beard hiding inside the helmet, making tackles anywhere and everywhere on the field. It appeared as though Bergey was the only defender the Eagles had on the field and, considering the kind of defenses he played with, that was often the case.

From 1974 to 1980 Bergey was Philly's middle linebacker and the heart, soul, and everything else of an Eagles defense that for most of that time couldn't stop anybody.

The irony, of course, was that once the Eagles did begin blossom into a formidable team, Bergey was reaching the end of his career and could not contribute in the way he once did. "I have no regrets," he said while announcing his retirement. "My only complaint is, the 12 years went too darn fast."

Bergey didn't start out as an Eagle. He was originally drafted by the Cincinnati Bengals in the second round of the 1969 draft and slipped into the starting lineup seamlessly, playing five quality seasons for the expansion franchise. But in 1974 he signed a deal with the upstart World Football League, enraging Bengals owner Paul Brown, who wanted to deal him to the Eagles for two first-round picks and a second-rounder. As it happened, the WFL folded soon after that and Bergey's contract was voided, meaning he was the Eagles' property after all.

And all he did with the Eagles was earn All-Pro honors four times, set a club record for most interceptions by a linebacker, earn team MVP honors three times, and help lift the Eagles from a laughingstock to a legitimate title contender. "I had so much to prove," Bergey said. "I wanted to show the Bengals what a horrible mistake they made, letting me go. And I wanted to show the Eagles I was worth what they paid for me."

Bergey did that—and more. In his first 10 NFL seasons, Bergey missed just two games due to injury, but in 1979—as the Eagles posted an 11–5 record and reached the second round of the play-offs—he suffered a serious knee injury that forced him to miss the end of that season, including the playoffs.

By 1980 he was 35 and knew he was at the end of his career, even without the injury he needed to rehabilitate. But he soldiered through, reclaimed his spot in the middle of the Eagles defense, and led them to their first Super Bowl. He had reached his goal of getting to the playoffs and the Super Bowl, but even he knew he couldn't play anymore. As it turned out, Super Bowl XV would be his last game, and he left with class and dignity. In 1988 he was enshrined in the Eagles Honor Roll.

He was also one of only five players who was with the Eagles at their worst, a 4–10 debacle in 1975, and stayed around long enough to see them reach the pinnacle five years later. "It was worth it," he said.

He did some radio work for the team and still helps out with broadcasts on occasion. He lives in Pennsylvania and remains an Eagles fan to this day.

70 Norm Willey's 17 Sacks

In the 1950s there was no such thing as a quarterback sack. In the 1950s there was no such thing as a celebratory dance when a quarterback was tackled. In the 1950s no one really thought much about it when a quarterback was tackled behind the line of scrimmage. In the 1950s tackling the quarterback as he was about to pass was just part of the job—no name, no number, no celebrity, and certainly no statistic.

History tells us that the term *quarterback sack* was first coined in the early 1970s by Los Angeles Rams defensive end Deacon Jones, and it didn't become an official NFL statistic until 1982. In fact, it really didn't seep into the NFL consciousness until later in the decade when every defensive player wanted credit for one— whether they really deserved it or not.

But if there had been such a thing as the quarterback sack in the 1950s, the best of the bunch would likely have been Eagles defensive end Norm "Wildman" Willey. In his eight years with the Eagles from 1950 to 1957, Willey estimates he averaged perhaps 20 sacks a season, and no one who watched him would necessarily disagree. "He was a terror," said Detroit Lions halfback Doak Walker. "He was in our backfield on every play."

That was never more true than on October 26, 1952, when Willey, unofficially at least, set an NFL record for most sacks in a game. No one really knew it at the time, and it was only chronicled by several newspaper accounts, and even those didn't make much of an issue about it.

On that day at the Polo Grounds, Willey dropped New York Giants quarterback Charlie Conerly 17 times on plays that would, today, be called sacks. Incredibly, in one sequence, he sacked Conerly on 11 straight plays.

"I almost feel sorry for Charlie," Eagles coach Jim Trimble said later. "He was just mauled by Norm. I had a fight with the Giants' chaplain after the game because he felt we were abusing Charlie Conerly. We had an argument going off the field."

If there had been statistics kept, Willey would own the sack mark by a substantial margin; the modern NFL record is just seven, set in 1990 by Kansas City Chiefs linebacker Derrick Thomas.

In 1956 Willey suffered a broken leg that took away his greatest advantage: speed. He played one more season but retired in 1957 and spent the next 20 seasons working field security at Eagles games.

Even Willey admitted he wishes there had been more defensive statistics kept in his day. "I'd like to see those 17 sacks in the record book," he said. "Any time you hold a record, people remember you."

Willey, who died in 2011, is certainly remembered, especially after being named to the Eagles' All-Star 75th Anniversary Team.

71 Bobby Walston

Ask any serious Eagles fans who the team's all-time leading scorer is, and the answer is easy: kicker David Akers. But who's No. 2? The answer may not come quite so easily, because it requires a serious trip back in Eagles history.

Bobby Walston is not a name that comes easily to the minds of Eagles fans, but during his career, which spanned from 1951 to 1962, he was as reliable a player as could be found in the NFL. He was from that era where players had more than one job, and he did his better than most.

Walston, a 14th-round draft out of the University of Georgia in 1951, was a sure-handed tight end who caught 311 passes and averaged more than 17 yards per catch, still among the Eagles' all-time leaders. He also caught 46 touchdown passes, which also remains one of the best in team history.

He was also a quality kicker who led the league with 114 points in 1954—at a time when the season was just 12 games long. He was the NFL Rookie of the Year in 1951 and was the league's second all-time leading scorer when he retired in 1962.

"Bobby Walston was the best draft pick I ever made," Eagles general manager Vince McNally said later. "We drafted him more for kicking than anything because he could kick the hell out of the ball. The fact that Bobby blossomed into a great receiver was a bonus."

Walston was also known for his toughness and his rather eclectic pursuits, which included an off-season job as a deputy sheriff in rural Georgia, his career as a collegiate boxing champ, and his certification as a deep-water diver. He missed only one game dating all the way back to his days of playing high school football.

In 1954 he broke his jaw during a game and was advised by doctors to sit and rest for at least three weeks. Walston would have none of it. He borrowed a pair of pliers, removed the wires that attached his busted jaw, and played the following week with a homemade brace of gauze and tape.

Even in his final season in 1962, after he broke his arm, Walston continued his duties as place kicker, booting the ball despite wearing a sling.

Walston stayed in football after his retirement, working as a scout for the Chicago Bears and in the USFL. In 1987 he died of a heart attack.

72 Leonard Tose

Just about everything with Leonard Tose was a gamble. It's what allowed him to buy the Eagles from Jerry Wolman in 1969, it's what allowed him to build a Super Bowl contender in the late 1970s and, ultimately, it's what forced him to sell the team in 1985. But it was one hell of a ride.

Dick Vermeil, one of the head coaches Tose hired, perhaps said it best at the former owner's eulogy after his death in 2003: "Leonard Tose was an original piece of work." Few would argue that point.

He lived life with flash, never thinking twice about taking his private helicopter (adorned with silver Eagles wings) down to Acapulco for a spur-of-the-moment vacation because, "It was faster."

The beginning of the end. Leonard Tose smokes a cigarette toward the end of his tenure as owner of the Eagles, probably contemplating his myriad poor business decisions.

He was always impeccably dressed and always seeking the finest things in life, which may have been one of the reasons he and his fourth wife (he was married five times) bought matching Rolls-Royces.

He was a Philadelphia native and grew to love the Eagles and was one of the 100 Brothers who bought shares in the team in 1949. Tose made his money in the family trucking business and tried to buy the Eagles in 1963. But at that time, he was outbid by Jerry Wolman, who six years later finally sold the team to Tose for $16.1 million, a record price for a professional sports franchise at that time. From there, Tose made the Eagles his personal plaything.

He wasted no time firing coach and general manager Joe Kuharich, persuading former Eagles great Pete Retzlaff to take over as GM. Retzlaff, in turn, hired Jerry Williams as the new head coach.

Over the next seven years, the Eagles went through another general manager and two more head coaches (Ed Khayat and Mike McCormack) before Tose found Dick Vermeil at UCLA. In 1976 Vermeil took over, and by 1978, the Eagles had their first winning record since 1966. Two years later, the Eagles were in the Super Bowl, and no one was happier than their eccentric owner.

That was the high point of the Tose era. By 1982 the players' strike hit, and Tose was deep in the hole from gambling losses, many of which he couldn't even remember.

By 1984 Tose's debt, which was estimated to be in the neighborhood of $42 million, led to serious thoughts of moving the franchise to Phoenix, Arizona, to take advantage of a new revenue-producing stadium and generous tax breaks. But Tose backed out, unable to bring himself to move his beloved Eagles. But he also knew at that stage that he was going to lose the team.

In 1985 Tose sold the team to Norman Braman for $65 million. After his debt was settled, he netted $10 million. "I made every mistake you could make," Tose lamented later.

Tose spiraled down after that, eventually being evicted from his Philadelphia mansion and living in a hotel room paid for by friends, including Vermeil.

Tose indeed made a lot of mistakes, though no one could deny his love for the team, and many players talked about his selfless acts of generosity that no one ever knew about.

Though there were hundreds of Leonard Tose stories, perhaps one in particular exemplified the nature of his relationship with his team. Before a 1972 game against the New York Giants, Tose tried to offer his struggling team some encouragement, predicting the Eagles would win the game, a comment that made its way into the Giants locker room. New York won 62–10, handing the Eagles their worst loss in 40 years. "I'll never do that again," Tose said afterward.

He was, indeed, an original piece of work.

73 Jon Runyan

In a 2008 poll among NFL players, the sight of Philadelphia Eagles tackle Jon Runyan coming at them to throw a block on a screen pass was voted one of the scariest things any of them could imagine. In a *Sports Illustrated* poll two years earlier, NFL players had voted Jon Runyan the second-dirtiest player in the league. Perhaps the two polls had something in common.

From the late 1990s to the early 2000s, Runyan was one of the meanest, biggest, and most effective offensive linemen in the NFL. He was also one of the highest paid.

Originally a fourth-round draft pick of the Houston Oilers in 1996 (they moved to Tennessee the following year), the 6'7",

330-pound University of Michigan product was a mainstay on the offensive line that helped the Titans reach the Super Bowl in 1999.

But in 2000 Eagles coach Andy Reid thought Runyan was exactly what he needed for his offense. The result? Philadelphia invested $30 million over six years to sign the free agent, making Runyan the highest-paid offensive lineman in the league.

"Jon brings an attitude to an offensive line," Reid said at the time. That phrase could mean anything. But in Reid's vernacular, it meant tough, nasty, and relentless—qualities Reid was convinced his line lacked.

The Eagles installed Runyan at right tackle and, literally, for the next 10 seasons he didn't leave, eventually starting 208 straight games (including his time with Houston/Tennessee).

Along the way, Runyan's reputation as a dirty player grew and, as a throwback to players from an earlier era, Runyan didn't necessarily argue the point. "I play the game the way it's supposed to be played," he said.

Runyan was a power blocker who thrived on blowing defensive linemen off the ball and making sure they stayed off the ball. That suited his game perfectly in Tennessee, but under Reid's West Coast offense, there was more of a reliance on pass-blocking. Runyan adapted, but he didn't necessarily like it and more than once asked Reid to run the ball more.

He played well enough to earn his only Pro Bowl berth in 2002 and then signed a contract extension after that season to ensure the Eagles would have the kind of stability they needed on the offensive line. In 2009 injuries reared up, and he finally retired.

But he almost immediately went into another career and in 2010 was elected as a Republican congressman to the U.S. House of Representatives in the Third Congressional District of New Jersey. He chose not to seek re-election in 2014 and was soon hired by the NFL as the vice president of the Policy and Rules Administration.

74 Troy Vincent

For a period in the late 1990s, the Philadelphia Eagles featured a defensive secondary that could be compared to the Bermuda Triangle: receivers went in but rarely came out—at least not with the football.

It was mostly due to a trio of tough, smart, hard-hitting players that included safety Brian Dawkins and cornerbacks Bobby Taylor and Troy Vincent. Longtime NFL observers would say Vincent may well have been the most complete, most vital element in that secondary that eventually combined for nine Pro Bowl appearances and 68 interceptions.

Vincent, a native of Trenton, New Jersey, who became a college star for a bad University of Wisconsin program, signed with the Eagles in 1996 after four seasons with the Miami Dolphins. For the next eight seasons, Vincent anchored the Eagles' secondary, intercepting 28 passes and earning five-straight Pro Bowl berths from 1999 to 2003. "I've learned so much from him," Taylor once said.

Vincent provided a calming influence and a professional attitude that seemed to rub off on everyone he played with. It was no coincidence then that in the 13 seasons he played, he was named a team captain 12 times, including all of his seasons with the Eagles.

Following the 2003 season, the Eagles chose not to re-sign Vincent, and he hooked on for one season with the Buffalo Bills and then with the Washington Redskins before retiring. But he will clearly be most remembered for his years with the Eagles, and in 2008 he was named to the Eagles' 75th Anniversary Team.

But as good as Vincent was on the field, he may have made more of a reputation off the field. In 2010 he was named vice president of the NFLPA player-development program, and he has taken a keen interest in making sure rookies invest their money properly so they don't face bankruptcy. In addition, in 2002 he was the Walter Payton NFL Man of the Year for his charitable work off the field.

In 2014 he was named the NFL's head of football operations. Still, there is talk among some of his fans that he is considering running for political office one day. It's talk Vincent hasn't necessarily shut down.

75 Joe Scarpati's Theft

Joe Scarpati, a cornerback of small stature but with huge heart, is probably best known for three things: the regret Vince Lombardi felt cutting him from the Packers in 1964, being the holder for Tom Dempsey's 63-yard field goal in 1970, and for "the theft."

Longtime Eagles fans know that last one best. So do longtime Dallas Cowboys fans. It turned out to be the most incredible play in a contest that some people still call the craziest game the Eagles have ever played.

It was November 6, 1966, at Franklin Field, and the Eagles, who had been embarrassed 56–7 by the Cowboys a month earlier, were desperately hanging on to a 24–23 lead in the final minute. But it didn't look good for the home team, who had scored all three of their touchdowns on kick returns—two kickoff returns by Timmy Brown and one punt return by Aaron Martin.

The Cowboys offense had moved up and down the field but could not score consistently, and the Eagles offense had managed just five first downs. So in the final minute, the Cowboys were inexorably moving down the field on the way to a last-second victory. On first down from the Philly 36, Cowboys quarterback Don Meredith threw a pass to halfback Dan Reeves, who shook off Scarpati's tackle and headed toward the goal line. Reeves could have stepped out of bounds to save time, but he didn't.

Instead, he cut back to the middle of the field, and Eagles cornerback Jim Nettles grabbed him at the 13-yard line and tried to bring him down. Scarpati, despite the missed tackle, never gave up on the play and roared back downfield, instinctively grabbing the ball from Reeves' arm. "The ball was right there," Scarpati said later. "I just reached in and grabbed it."

Scarpati saw the official had a whistle in his mouth and was ready to blow the play dead before the takeaway—but he didn't. "A split second later would have been too late," Scarpati said.

A stunned Reeves looked around for the whistle that never came, and Scarpati headed back upfield before he was knocked out of bounds.

Even the perpetrator of the theft was sure it was illegal until the referee spotted the ball for play. Meanwhile Reeves was screaming in protest, knocking over an official on the way and earning the only ejection of his career.

The "fumble recovery" sealed Philly's win, and the Eagles went on to win four of their last five games and finish with a solid 9–5 record, their first winning record since 1961.

To this day, Reeves contends the play was illegal, though they both joke about it now. "The guy's been to, like, 20 Super Bowls and he still remembers that play," Scarpati said. "It must have been pretty good."

76 Stan Walters

There was a time when Stan Walters was considered too passive to be a great left tackle.

He had the size—6'6", 275 pounds—which in the mid-1970s was gargantuan. He had the pedigree, having played at Syracuse University. But he was missing...something.

In 1973 he was a ninth-round draft pick of the Cincinnati Bengals, but was just a part-time starter. In 1975 he was dealt to the Eagles, and in 1976 new coach Dick Vermeil let the five-year veteran know the facts of life in training camp: get better or get gone. "That definitely shook me up," Walters said.

And from that point on, he became the player everyone thought he could be. In fact, he would go on to start 122 straight games, reach two Pro Bowls, help the Eagles to their first Super Bowl, and earn induction into the Eagles Honor Roll. Not bad for a guy who didn't think he was much of a football player in the first place. "I didn't love football," he said later. "My game was basketball."

But Walters had the size and athleticism to become a terrific left tackle, even if he really didn't have the temperament. Walters was more interested in talking about books and politics and current events as opposed to the defensive end who opposed him. And the violent NFL culture? That amused him more than anything else. "The rookies would yell, 'Yeah! Kill! Kill!'" Walter recalled. "I just laughed. You don't kill anybody out there, and if you think that's what you have to do, you've got a lot to learn."

But on game day, few tackles did their job as well as Walters. One rival defensive end, the Dallas Cowboys' inimitable Harvey Martin, called Walters the smartest tackle in the NFL.

And Vermeil, who all but threatened Walters with his release that first year, came to be one of his biggest backers, crediting Walters with helping change the culture of the football team. "He was a big-game performer," Vermeil said years later. "He was like a college professor playing football."

Walters played through the 1983 season, then went to the radio booth, joining play-by-play announcer Merrill Reese on Eagles broadcasts for the next 14 years. He's now retired from broadcasting and lives in the Atlanta area.

77 Duce Staley

You always knew when Duce Staley was carrying the football. If you closed your eyes and listened, you could hear the thunderous "Duuuuuce!" reverberating through the crowd. It was his trademark, and it always made him smile. "I work hard and I run hard," Staley said once. "I think that's why fans relate to me. I'm a blue-collar guy like them."

He was surely that, but he was a lot more. A third-round Eagles draft pick in 1997 from the University of South Carolina, Staley followed the model of a number of Eagles draft choices of the era: small and tough and with a chip the size of Montana on his shoulder. They were guys who were told they should not and would not succeed in the NFL and then set about proving everyone wrong. At 5'10" and 200 pounds, Staley was no different. "I'm proud of the fact that I overcame a lot," Staley said.

He spent his rookie season backing up Ricky Watters at running back while contributing big-time on special teams, leading the team in kickoff returns as well as in special-teams tackles.

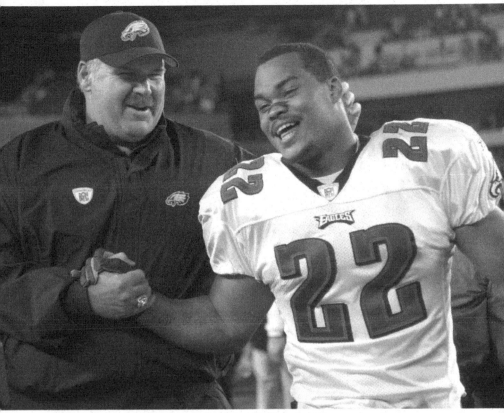

Eagles head coach Andy Reid, left, celebrates their 27–25 win over the Washington Redskins with running back Duce Staley on October 5, 2003 at the newly opened Linc in Philly.

By 1998 Watters was gone, and the starting tailback job was his. He responded with 1,065 rushing yards and 57 receptions, despite playing most of the season with a hernia.

But in 1999 everything changed. Ray Rhodes was out as head coach, and Andy Reid, a true believer in the self-styled West Coast offense, was in. The new regime both benefited and, in the end, hurt Staley's performance in Philadelphia.

Initially, it was Reid's belief in Staley as a versatile, every-down back that led to the decision not to draft Heisman Trophy–winning running back Ricky Williams and pick quarterback Donovan McNabb instead. "Duce is just so versatile," Reid said. "He can catch the ball as well as run it. And he can run inside and outside, and you don't see many backs his size running inside as well as he does."

Staley justified Reid's faith in him by running for 1,273 yards and catching 41 passes. Staley accounted for 1,567 total yards that season, 41 percent of the Eagles' offensive output. No player had ever been that involved in the offense before.

Staley continued to produce, running for 201 yards in the 2000 season opener against the Cowboys. But an injury a few weeks later ended his season and nearly his career. Two bones in his right foot were dislocated, and the rehab process would be difficult and painful. Indeed, some thought he might not play again because no one could imagine a worse injury for a running back.

But he was back the next season and led the Eagles in rushing and tied for the team lead with 63 receptions out of the backfield. He was also awarded the NFL Players Association Ed Block Courage Award for his public service.

He added another 1,029 rushing yards in 2002, but in 2003, Reid opted to go with a rotation system at running back that included Staley, Correll Buckhalter, and Brian Westbrook. And while his overall numbers dropped, he had one of his most productive seasons while tutoring the younger backs along the way.

But Staley was unhappy with the system, and after the Eagles lost to the Carolina Panthers in the NFC Championship Game that season, he signed a free-agent deal with the Pittsburgh Steelers.

Staley's 4, 807 career rushing yards are still fourth in team history behind only Wilbert Montgomery, Westbrook, and Steve Van Buren.

He decided to retire after the 2006 season, and in an emotional ceremony at halftime of the Eagles-Giants game on December 9, 2007, Staley officially retired as an Eagle.

He went into radio work and in 2010, anxious to get back into the game that had treated him so well, he rejoined the Eagles as special-teams quality-control coach and in 2013 became the team's running backs coach.

78 Otho Davis

He was a combination of trainer, psychiatrist, friend, practical joker, and trusted adviser. Otho Davis' title may have been head trainer of the Philadelphia Eagles for 23 seasons, but to the hundreds of players he treated, befriended, and commiserated with, he was a lot more than that.

"I feel as if every player is a part of me," Davis told *Sports Illustrated* once. "Unless you feel that, you can't get close, you can't relate to the player. We cut up and joke. But deep down, there's seriousness on both sides. We're all devoted to one another."

All most football fans see of a trainer are the times during a game when he sprints on to the field to tend to an injured player. But that's only a fraction of the real duties that include hours of tedious work in the training room with a player who may, Davis sometimes knows, never play again.

"Football players are supposed to be so tough," running back Wilbert Montgomery told *Sports Illustrated*. "We try not to let anybody know how much we hurt or how scared we are. But you can't fool Otho. He senses it." And from 1973 until his retirement after the 1995 season, few were better at the job than Davis.

There were hundreds, perhaps thousands, of times over the years when Davis would stay with a player for as long as it took to rehab an injury. Quarterback Ron Jaworski recalled one time when he sprained an ankle in a game in Detroit. "We got back from the game, and Otho worked on my ankle until 2:00 AM." Jaworksi said. "The next day he was back at 7:00 AM, and he massaged my foot for three hours. I couldn't even touch it, but he worked miracles." Jaworksi played the following Sunday.

Davis was also known as a top-flight, first-class practical joker, another example of how he kept players loose in a profession when the next play could be there last. He would get anyone, anywhere, whether it was rookie free agent or an All-Pro veteran. "We can't do anything to get Otho," Montgomery once said. "We live in fear."

Even on his office door, Davis would announce what was to come: *Posted...Protected Area...The Otho Davis Wildlife Sanctuary.*

"He's the best," Montgomery said.

Davis got his start as a trainer at the college level, working at Kent State and Duke University before joining the Baltimore Colts and then heading to the Eagles. It was in Philadelphia where his reputation as a trainer grew. Not only did he employ all of the state-of-the-art equipment that helped players recover quicker, he was known as the trainer every player could trust. He was NFL Trainer of the Year five times, was inducted into the Athletic Trainers Hall of Fame in 1981, and is still being touted by many people for induction into the Pro Football Hall of Fame.

Trainers today still model their treatment regimen on what Davis did, and many of them say they got into the business because of him.

After the 1995 season, Davis retired back to his home in Texas and in 2000 died of pancreatic cancer.

79 Bobby Taylor

When the Eagles traded up in the second round of the 1995 draft to take Notre Dame cornerback Bobby Taylor, the organization was effectively announcing a drastic shift in philosophy. The days of the small, tough cover guys were over. In Taylor, the Eagles had a 6'3", 215-pounder, huge for a cornerback in the mid-1990s. But the move was made out of necessity to counter the tall, angular wide receivers that were becoming the rage of NFL offenses. "We're lucky to get this kid," coach Ray Rhodes said at the time.

Even today, the jury is out on just how good Taylor was. He played nine seasons for the Eagles, battling big receivers every week. There was also some question about his toughness, and Eagles fans squawked often about the number of his missed tackles. But he made plays when they needed to be made, and he did earn a Pro Bowl berth in 2002.

Rhodes wasted little time throwing Taylor into the fire, inserting him on the starting lineup midway through his rookie season. It was a game in December of that year in which Taylor showed flashes of what he could do as he held Cowboys All-Pro receiver Michael Irvin to three meaningless catches in an Eagles win. That performance earned Taylor NFC Defensive Player of the Week honors.

Taylor also excelled in the playoffs that year. Again, he was NFC Defensive Player of the Week.

And for the next eight years, Taylor was a stalwart on the corner, more often than not drawing the coverage assignment on the opposition's best receiver. Taylor found himself on the proverbial "island" often, especially when Jim Johnson was hired as defensive coordinator and employed dozens of exotic blitz packages. Those packages forced cornerbacks into a lot of one-on-one coverages and, frankly, left Taylor open to allow big plays. And there were more than a few of them that left some fans puzzled.

In 2003, a year after his first Pro Bowl berth, Taylor missed nine games with a foot injury. He returned in time for the Eagles' NFC Championship Game loss to the Carolina Panthers but decided it was time to move on. He signed a free-agent deal with the Seattle Seahawks but couldn't gain a starting role and retired. In 2010, at age 36 and having been away from the game for six seasons, he sent tapes to every NFL team in hopes of making a comeback.

There were no takers. He's now living in Houston and is studying to become a sports agent.

80 Seth Joyner

It was January 1998, and Seth Joyner finally smiled. He was standing on the podium at a Super Bowl media feeding frenzy in San Diego, and the veteran linebacker had reached the promised land—his promised land.

Earlier that year, when the Green Bay Packers signed Joyner as a free agent from the Arizona Cardinals, Packers coach Mike Holmgren had joked with Joyner, "Don't you ever smile?" Joyner replied, "I'll smile when I get to a Super Bowl."

Now he was finally there—albeit in a backup role. And even after the game, when the Packers were upset by the Denver Broncos, there was a serenity about Joyner. He had reached his goal. Little did he know that the following season, as a backup with the Broncos, he'd have even more to revel in when Denver beat the Atlanta Falcons for their second straight Super Bowl title.

Seth Joyner in game action against the New Orleans Saints on October 13, 1991, at the Vet.

With nothing else to attain, Joyner retired, content and complete after 13 tough NFL seasons. But before that, there had been his turbulent and impressive career that began with the Eagles, where he made a name for himself as one of the game's best linebackers.

Joyner, one of just 11 players who finished his career with at least 20 interceptions (24) and 20 sacks (52) was an eighth-round draft pick for the Eagles in 1986 from Texas-El Paso and was actually cut in training camp before being re-signed when another linebacker was injured. Coach Buddy Ryan inserted him in the starting lineup midway through the 1986 season, and he never left.

He then became an integral part of defensive coordinator Bud Carson's swarming defense, and his versatility made him an every-down player. But Joyner also came into the NFL during the golden era of NFL linebackers, when the New York Giants' Lawrence Taylor and the New Orleans' Saints' Pat Swilling and the Kansas City Chiefs' Derrick Thomas and Chicago's Mike Singletary were all at their raging best.

Joyner was caught in the backwash and didn't attain the notoriety of some other linebackers. But it's generally considered that his "coming out party" was a December 1991 *Monday Night Football* game in Houston against the Oilers.

In that game, Joyner played with a 102-degree fever but in the end made the powerful Oilers sick. Joyner recorded eight solo tackles, forced two fumbles, recovered two fumbles, and posted two quarterback sacks—all in front of a national TV audience.

"I've been sick for a week," Joyner said afterward. "My stomach was bubbling. It was hard to breathe. But you have to play." For many football fans, it was the first real look at the intimidating, scowling Joyner.

He was named the NFL Defensive Player of the Year by *Sports Illustrated* and earned his first of three Pro Bowl nods that year.

But Joyner cared little for the individual accolades—what he wanted was a title, and those eluded him in Philadelphia. By 1993 he was frustrated with the Eagles and coach Rich Kotite, whom he found uninspiring, even labeling the coach a "puppet" of owner Norman Braman.

Joyner left after that season and played three seasons with the Arizona Cardinals, where he remained one of the NFL's best linebackers. He then spent 1997 in Green Bay, where he finally got to the Super Bowl, and 1998 with the Broncos, where he finally won one.

Since then he did some coaching but is now a football analyst for FS1.

81 Vince Papale

Even the most casual Philadelphia Eagles fan knows about Vince Papale. Maybe fact and myth merge on occasion regarding what he really did in his remarkable three seasons with the Eagles, but everyone knows about his rags-to-riches story that earned him the nickname "Rocky" among his teammates.

He was a schoolteacher who had never played college football. But when the opportunity presented itself to play the game he loved, Papale was not only in the right place at the right time, he seized the opportunity with both hands. "Most people thought I was nuts," Papale said later. "Fortunately for me, Dick Vermeil wasn't one of them."

This much must be understood: Papale was no slouch athletically. He was 6'2", weighed 195 pounds, and had competed as a decathlete and pole vaulter while attending St. Joseph's College.

After college he became a high school teacher and coach and played in a two-hand-touch football league on the weekends.

Curious to see if he could move to the next level, he played for a local semipro tackle team, the Aston Knights, where he proved to be one of the league's dominant players. Then his ambitions really took off.

Invincible

Hollywood has never let the truth get in the way of a good story. And that was certainly the case with the 2006 film *Invincible*, based on Vince Papale's improbable story.

Produced by Disney Studios, which has done its share of sports movies, from *The Rookie* to *Remember the Titans*, *Invincible* came out in August 2006 and struck a chord with moviegoers, grossing nearly $58 million at the box office.

Mark Wahlberg starred as Papale, and the film received considerable support from both the player himself (in fact, his two children had bit parts) and the Eagles, who knew a public-relations gold mine when they saw one.

Some of the story depicted was even true. It chronicled Papale's days as a schoolteacher and bartender in Philly, though it did leave out the fact that he was already a great athlete who had played professionally for the Philadelphia Bell of the World Football League.

And in the dramatic finale, it shows Papale scoring a touchdown after recovering a fumble against the Giants. He did indeed recover the fumble, but the fumble was ruled a muff by officials, and the ball could not be advanced. In truth, Papale never scored an NFL touchdown and caught only one pass—the last NFL completion by Roman Gabriel.

The scenes at what was supposed to be Veterans Stadium were actually filmed at Franklin Field, and computer graphics filled in the blanks.

Still, the story was warm-hearted and inspiring and did wonders not only for Papale's legacy but for the Eagles organization.

The World Football League formed in 1974, and Philadelphia had a franchise that was holding open auditions for players. Papale made the team and eventually became a starting wide receiver.

A few months after the WFL folded in October 1975, Papale contacted new Eagles coach Dick Vermeil, who was intrigued. He was looking for hungry, enthusiastic players who would energize the lethargic atmosphere in the Eagles locker room.

And though Papale was 30, ancient in NFL terms, Vermeil gave him a private tryout and invited him to training camp in 1976.

Papale made the team and played in 41 of 44 games over the next three seasons, almost exclusively on special teams. In that time, he recovered two fumbles, including one in just his second game, which led to a win over the New York Giants.

In 1978 Papale was voted special-teams captain by his teammates as well as Philadelphia Man of the Year for his charitable activities. Along the way, he became a true fan favorite. "The blue-collar guys in the upper deck loved it when I hit a first-round draft pick," he said. "They felt like they got a piece of that rich so-and-so too."

But a shoulder injury ended the dream, and in 1979 he retired, still a die-hard Eagles fan. "All I asked for was a fair shot, and I got one," Papale said.

He worked in TV and as a radio broadcaster for a few years after that and is now a commercial mortgage banker still living in the Philly area.

And even today, fans recognize him and thank him for what he did for little guys and dreamers everywhere.

82 Andre Waters

His nickname was "Dirty" and, while he hated the moniker, he also reveled in it. He knew what it meant, and so did every other player in the NFL. When Dirty Waters was patrolling the outer reaches of the defense from his strong safety spot, rival wide receivers knew what could be in store for them.

For a period in the late 1980s to the early 1990s, Andre Waters was one of the NFL's most feared tacklers. He was a heat-seeking missile, a game-changer and, in the minds of many, the dirtiest player in the NFL.

He is also yet another tragic example of what can happen in the NFL when head injuries are not diagnosed early enough. On November 20, 2006, Waters went outside his home in Tampa, Florida, and shot himself in the head. He was dead at age 44.

Doctors who examined his brain afterward said the deterioration in the tissue resembled that of a 90-year-old man in the throes of advanced dementia. "Football killed him," one of the doctors said.

Waters is another example of players from an earlier era who hit hard, leading with their heads and using their helmets as a weapon. Concussions were not treated as seriously then as they are now, and Waters once said he had no idea how many he suffered over the years.

But the tragic end to his life overshadowed what was a remarkable career for an overachiever who should never have played in the NFL but, through sheer will and determination, did anyway.

He earned a spot on the Eagles roster in 1984 as an undersized, undrafted free agent out of Cheyney State. But coach Marion

Campbell liked what he saw in the tough guy and put him on special teams, where he excelled.

In 1986, when Buddy Ryan took over as head coach, he was intrigued by how hard Waters hit and moved him to strong safety. "He's the kind of player who turns people upside-down and laughs at them," Ryan said at the time. It proved to be truer than he knew.

In short order, Waters' reputation for going after receivers over the middle, whether the ball was there or not, grew. He was known for knocking several players out of games, including Rams quarterback Jim Everett, whom Waters hit below the waist while Everett was throwing.

The NFL finally installed a rule, unofficially dubbed the Andre Waters Rule, that defenders could not hit quarterbacks below the waist then they were in the pocket and preparing to throw the ball.

Waters also shattered the ankle of Washington Redskins kicker Jess Atkinson by hitting him low, though Waters apologized every time he saw Atkinson in the future.

Indeed, Waters always insisted he never tried to hurt anyone. He said he was simply playing the game as hard as he could because he knew no other way.

Waters sparked the Eagles' infamous defenses of the late 1980s and early 1990s, defenses that played hard and well but were reputed to push just a little further than they needed to go.

Waters was the Eagles' leading tackler for four seasons, including three-straight from 1987 to 1989, and he intercepted 15 passes. But by 1994, Ryan was gone and Waters lost his starting spot to Michael Zordich. He was released and spent his last two seasons playing for Ryan in Arizona.

Waters then went into college coaching and had hoped to land a position with the Eagles but could not.

Friends said they saw nothing unusual in Waters in the days and weeks before his suicide. And while he left no note, family and friends are convinced brain damage from years of collisions went a long way toward his ultimate decision—a sad end to a remarkable career.

83 Mike Quick

By the time his nine-year career with the Eagles was over, Mike Quick had built some impressive numbers, including 363 career receptions, 6,464 receiving yards, 61 touchdown receptions, and five trips to the Pro Bowl. But imagine how much better those statistics could have been had he avoided some circumstances that proved to be out of his control.

In a five-year period from 1983 to 1987, there were few receivers better than Mike Quick. Still, injuries cut short what could well have been a Hall of Fame career, had it lasted longer. But Quick, now the color analyst for the Eagles Radio Network, has no regrets. "Pro football has worked out far beyond my wildest dreams," he once said.

That he ended up an Eagle in the first place was a twist of fate. In the first round of the 1982 draft, the Eagles had set their gaze on Clemson wide receiver Perry Tuttle. But the Buffalo Bills wanted him too and traded up to take Tuttle with the 19th pick, one ahead of the Eagles.

Shocked by the turn of events, the Eagles retrenched and went with who they saw as the second-best receiver in the draft, North Carolina State's Mike Quick. It proved to be a prophetic move. Tuttle flamed out after three nondescript seasons, while Quick became one of the game's best wideouts. "It all worked out," Quick said.

But his opportunity came slowly, mostly because of the 1982 players strike that cancelled nearly half of the season. But in 1983 he blossomed, leading the league (and setting a club record) with 1,409 receiving yards and 13 touchdowns, which tied a team record last set by Tommy McDonald in 1961.

That began his run of five-straight trips to the Pro Bowl, leading all NFL wide receivers in touchdowns (53) and piling up 5,437 yards, trailing only future Hall of Famers James Lofton and Steve Largent.

He is perhaps best known for what he accomplished in a November 1985 game in Philadelphia against the Atlanta Falcons. Sitting on his own 1-yard line in overtime, quarterback Ron Jaworski stepped back and threw a bullet to a slanting Quick over the middle. Quick gathered in the pass between two defenders and accelerated. He was never touched, and the 99-yard touchdown pass remains the longest in team history and just one of six times that has occurred in NFL history.

But in 1988, when Quick should have been hitting the peak of his career, injuries began to pile up. In the eighth week of that year, Quick broke his leg and was lost for the rest of the season. The next season, Quick played just six games before a knee injury ended his season. Injuries again plagued him in 1990, and it was at that stage he decided he'd had enough. "I keep hoping I will wake up and it will feel better, but it doesn't," he said at his retirement press conference.

But a chance trip in the Eagles' radio booth during one of his injuries allowed Quick to look toward the future. He proved to be a natural as a color commentator and has spent the past 23 years working with Merrill Reese on Eagles games.

84 Franklin Field

Perhaps Bert Bell, who knew as much about the Philadelphia Eagles franchise as anyone, said it best. With the benefit of a few years and a little hindsight, Bell said the Eagles' move from decaying Shibe Park/Connie Mack Stadium in 1958 to Franklin Field "saved pro football for Philadelphia." It was not an overstatement.

The Eagles had been around several decades and even had a couple of NFL titles to their name. But the team was still little more than a regional obsession. Eagles games drew maybe 20,000 fans, and that wasn't enough to sustain long-term health. Knowing they needed to leave Shibe Park, where they had played for 18 years, the Eagles focused on the much larger Franklin Field on the campus of Penn University.

The move was officially announced January 20, 1958, and both sides seemed to get a good deal from it. The Eagles did not have to pay rent because of the nonprofit status of the university but would pay for maintenance and other expenses, which was reportedly between $75,000 and $100,000 per year, far less than they were paying before. Meanwhile, the university would receive revenue from all concessions and parking.

The Eagles now had a stadium with a more-than-60,000-seat capacity, nearly twice the capacity of their previous venue, and the parking issues that had plagued fans coming to the game were also gone.

The Eagles were now the only team in the NFL to play all their home games at a college stadium, and everyone seemed happy with it. Indeed, in 1962, when city officials approached the Eagles about building a new multipurpose stadium, the team politely declined,

Franklin Field played host to the 1960 NFL Championship Game, seen here. The game was a 17–13 victory over the Green Bay Packers on December 26, 1960.

citing a poll saying that 80 percent of Eagles season-ticket holders preferred Franklin Field.

As for the product on the field, it was a decidedly mixed bag. In their 13 years playing there, the Eagles compiled a 41–45–2 record, though they did win the 1960 NFL Championship Game there, beating the Green Bay Packers in front of a packed house.

Tragically, the next season, Bert Bell, who had been such an advocate for the move, suffered a heart attack in the stands and died while watching his team beat the Steelers. By the late 1960s, the fate of the Eagles at Franklin Field was already sealed when construction began downtown on the new multipurpose Veterans Stadium.

The Eagles played their final game at Franklin Field on December 20, 1970, and defeated the Steelers 30–20. As the game ended, the two last-place teams engaged in a brawl.

Perhaps it was a fitting ending.

85 Marion Campbell

As a head coach, Marion Campbell turned out to be a terrific assistant coach. It's not all that unusual. The NFL is littered with great assistant coaches who felt the next logical step for them was to become a head coach. But too often, it never worked out, because being a head coach, and therefore taking responsibility for everything, bears little resemblance to being an assistant and taking charge of just one aspect of the process. Marion Campbell was a classic example of the phenomenon.

He was a highly respected and successful defensive coordinator for the Minnesota Vikings, Los Angeles Rams, Atlanta Falcons, and the Eagles, where he ran the defense for the 1980 Super Bowl team. But in nine seasons as a head coach, both with the Falcons and then with the Eagles from 1983 through 15 games of the 1985 season, Campbell never produced a winning season.

Even so, Campbell's football pedigree was unquestioned. A standout defensive lineman, he played for the Eagles from 1956 to 1961 and was a key member of the 1960 championship team. In 1964 he got his first chance to coach, joining the staff of Norm Van Brocklin in Minnesota.

By 1977 he had built his reputation as a defensive guru and Dick Vermeil, now in his second season of rebuilding the Eagles, hired Campbell to install his vaunted 3–4 defense. For the next few seasons, with Campbell running the show, the Eagles invariably had one of the best defenses in the NFL. But after the 1982 season, Vermeil made the surprising announcement that he was quitting, and Campbell slipped in as head coach.

Unfortunately for Campbell, he was taking over an Eagles team that was in turmoil. Team owner Leonard Tose was looking to sell the team, and the players who had been so instrumental in the Super Bowl were aging. But Campbell took the reins and did the best he could with what he had. The first season in 1983, the Eagles started 4–2 before losing nine of their last 10 games. In 1984 it wasn't much better as the Eagles stumbled to 6–9–1, losing three of their last four games.

By 1985 Norman Braman was in full control as owner, and the people Campbell had felt comfortable with were all gone. It was a recipe for disaster that unfolded spectacularly in a December 1985 home game against the Vikings.

Braman had invited the entire 1960 Eagles championship team to celebrate the 25th anniversary of the title. In all, 18 former players showed up to watch their old teammate coach the new Eagles.

Philly built a 23–0 lead with eight minutes to play, when Minnesota mounted its incredible comeback. A combination of poor coaching decisions, Eagles mistakes, and a rejuvenated Vikings offense erased the deficit, and as a Veterans Stadium crowd howled in fury, the Eagles lost 28–23. "That was probably the toughest loss I've been involved in since I've been in this business," Campbell said quietly. "I'm still numb."

Braman, who wasn't a huge Campbell fan anyway, was diplomatic afterward when asked about Campbell's future as the team's head coach. "You don't make any decisions based on the last eight minutes," he said. But inside, he seethed. This wasn't what he had expected from his new investment.

Matters became worse when the Eagles lost their next two games, dropping them out of playoff contention. By then,

Braman was ready to move on. He held secret talks with 26-year-old David Shula to see if he was interested in taking over. And Campbell could see what was happening too. He asked team brass for a quick decision, and he got it. The night the team got back from a loss in San Diego, he was fired, and defensive coordinator Fred Bruney took over for the last game—a 37–35 win over the Vikings.

But Campbell's players wouldn't let him go without making a small showing of their appreciation for him. In that game, they honored him by writing *Fox 78* on their shoes. *Fox* was for Campbell's nickname—the Swamp Fox—and 78 was the number he wore in his heyday as a player with the Eagles.

"I feel at peace," Campbell said in a press release after he was let go.

He was never a head coach again and, probably somewhere deep down inside, that was just fine with him.

Campbell died in July 2016.

86 Freddie Mitchell

Perhaps no player in team history has gotten more mileage from doing so little for so long. Love him or hate him, Freddie Mitchell was impossible to ignore.

A first-round draft choice out of UCLA for the Eagles in 2001, Mitchell never came close to living up to his potential—at least on the field. In his four seasons with the Eagles, he caught just 90 passes, but to hear him tell it, he was the best player on the field every time out. He was the same guy who at a press conference thanked his hands for being so great.

In truth, his only notable achievement as a player came in the January 11, 2004, NFC playoff game against the Packers when, facing fourth-and-26 late in the fourth quarter, Eagles quarterback Donovan McNabb connected with Mitchell for a 28-yard gain. Philly eventually won the game in overtime and went to the Super Bowl.

Actually, Mitchell just wasn't a very good receiver. He had trouble picking up the Eagles' intricate offense, and he didn't work all that hard to learn it. And, oh yeah, he never shut up.

In the week before the Super Bowl in 2005, Mitchell enraged normally stoic Patriots coach Bill Belichick by purposely forgetting the names of the New England defensive backs. Belichick shot back afterward, "I was happy when he was in the game because he's a terrible player."

Mitchell also frosted his teammates when, after the Super Bowl loss, he complained that he didn't get enough passes thrown his way. "I guess they didn't want to win the game," he said.

He was also the one to start the rumor that McNabb was throwing up in the huddle during the final drive. McNabb and everyone else in the huddle denied it ever happened.

The Eagles finally gave up on Mitchell and released him in the spring of 2005. He tried to latch on to the Kansas City Chiefs that season, but he never made it through training camp. He then tried to play for the Dallas Cowboys and Baltimore Ravens as well as Toronto of the Canadian Football League, all with no luck.

Out of football now, he has had his share of legal problems, including legal issues with a restaurant he owned in Florida. He was also sentenced to 37 months in prison in 2013 for non-payment of child support. Now out of prison, he remains a colorful and quotable character in the Philadelphia area. He may have been a wasted first-round draft pick, but Freddie Mitchell was nothing if not entertaining.

87 Wade Key

Wade Key meant a lot to the Philadelphia Eagles in the 10 seasons he played there.

Consider that the gregarious Texan, a 13th-round draft pick in 1969 from tiny Southwest Texas State University, started barely half the games he played. Yet when it came time to vote for the Eagles' All-Star 75th Anniversary Team in 2007, Key was among them. That's respect.

That's because he did whatever he was asked to do whenever he was asked to do it and did as well as he possibly could. "I just had a lot of fun playing," he said.

His tale was not atypical from other players who played at small schools and were relatively unknown. But Key was different in that he really wasn't sure if he wanted to play pro football in the first place.

He recounted a tale recently to the Eagles website: "During the draft, the [Los Angeles] Rams called me five or six times, and I kept telling them, 'Look, I don't want to be drafted. I want to finish my senior year and get my degree,'" he said. "Then I woke up the next morning, and I was drafted by the Eagles. I fretted over that for a while, and then you kind of get over it."

He was a star tight end in college who was moved to tackle by the Eagles. Worse than playing a new position, the guard next to him, a guy he needed to trust, kept changing. "There were four of them my first three years," Key said with a laugh. But he persevered.

In 1973 first-year head coach Mike McCormack moved him over to guard, and he flourished there. "I knew I'd found a home," Key said. "I probably always was destined to play guard because I wasn't that big. I was 250 pounds. I had a lot more quickness."

So Key settled into perhaps the most anonymous position on a football field, and he loved it. That first Eagles offense, sparked by Key, averaged 128 rushing yards per game, the team's best effort in years.

But they still weren't winning. In Key's first eight seasons, Philly didn't have a winning record. Then in 1978, in Dick Vermeil's third season, the Eagles posted a 9–7 record and earned a playoff spot. The following season, they won a wild-card berth with an 11–5 record and got to the second round of the playoffs.

"Dick was a hell of a coach," said Key, who should know since in his career he played for four different head coaches. "He surrounded himself with really great people, and they cared about us, and they worked with us, and it was a really, really good time."

But in February 1980 Key had surgery on his right hamstring to remove a calcium deposit and was still rehabbing the injury when training camp began. During camp, as Key was still getting healthy, Vermeil approached him and asked him if he could play left tackle during preseason to help protect valuable quarterback Ron Jaworski. Key, of course, agreed. But late in the preseason, Key was stunned when he was waived. "I couldn't figure out what happened because I wasn't even supposed to get on the field until September," he said.

But, as with everything else, Key handled with it with good humor and understanding, even though that was the season the Eagles reached their first Super Bowl. "It's gone, it's done, it's past," he said. "I had so much fun, and those people treated me so good."

Key has stayed in football, coaching high school in San Antonio and recalling a career he wasn't even sure he wanted.

"It was a fun time," he said simply.

88 Chip Kelly

For several years after it ended, the Eagles organization wanted to forget about the intriguing, but ultimately unsuccessful, experiment that was head coach Chip Kelly.

Kelly, the latest in the long line of coaches from the college ranks to earn the ill-fated moniker "offensive genius," was going to transform the Eagles from the plodding, disorganized group left by Andy Reid into a vibrant, exciting football maelstrom that would overwhelm the NFL.

His offenses, created in the far off Northwest at the University of Oregon, was otherworldly. His schemes featured smart, athletic players who could run anywhere and everywhere.

His legend really began at the University of New Hampshire from 1999 to 2006, when, as offensive coordinator, his teams averaged more than 400 yards per game. It continued when he was hired as offensive coordinator at Oregon before taking over as head coach in 2009. He took the Ducks to three straight Bowl Championship Series games, including the national championship game in 2010, with his philosophy that was known as the "blur offense."

By the end of the 2012 season, Kelly's was the hottest name in coaching and several NFL teams—including the Buffalo Bills, Cleveland Browns, and the Eagles—were looking to make a change.

In the end, Kelly took the Eagles' job and excitement, once again, washed over fans who believed this was a new beginning.

But, as with many experiments that started with so much promise, it ended in the disillusionment and frustration that is often the by-product of hubris.

Kelly indeed brought his kinetic offense to Philly and led a remarkable turnaround from 4-12 in 2012 to a 10-6 record and an NFC East title in 2013. What was more impressive was how he turned a relatively unknown quarterback, Nick Foles, into a star. In 13 games, Foles was poised and confident, completing 64 percent of his passes while throwing 27 touchdown passes and just two interceptions.

And while the Eagles duplicated that record in 2014, they missed the playoffs.

In 2015, Kelly added the role of personnel director to his title and made some trades that puzzled many. Nick Foles, his star quarterback from two years before, was sent to St. Louis, and All-Pro running back LeSean McCoy was traded to Buffalo.

Kelly's offense sputtered and the defense, which was rarely more than an afterthought to him, struggled. As well, Kelly's prickly personality began to wear on players, coaches, fans, and the front office. Finally, mired in a 6–9 season, Kelly was fired. Barely a month later, he was hired as head coach of the San Francisco 49ers, where he lasted just one season.

After a year away from football, Kelly returned to what he knew best and was hired in 2017 to take over at UCLA.

As for the Eagles, they hired the anti-Kelly in Doug Pederson, an amiable, smart coach who has melded beautifully with the organization.

Ironically, while Kelly is gone, he is hardly forgotten in Philadelphia. As the Eagles prepared for the NFC Championship Game against the Minnesota Vikings in 2017, Pederson and his staff were seeking ways to make quarterback Nick Foles feel more comfortable. So they went back through old video of his days when Kelly was his coach with the Eagles.

There they found the key, Using what has been become the latest NFL acronym, the RPO, or run/pass option, so favored by Kelly but which has been a staple of the game forever. The freedom of choosing the option to hand the ball off or throw it was what Foles did best, and loved most. And when the coaching staff decided to let Foles loose to make quick decisions that he favored, everything changed.

He played near flawlessly against the top-ranked Vikings and in the bright lights and crushing pressure of the Super Bowl, he was even better.

Chip Kelly may have rubbed many people the wrong way, but he gave Nick Foles the confidence and the opportunity to reach his potential as a quarterback.

And 3,000 miles away, Kelly, perhaps for the final time, has left his imprint on the Eagles.

89 Tommy Thompson

He was partially blind in one eye, and he missed two crucial years in his career because of service in World War II, but Tommy Thompson remains one of the great quarterbacks in Eagles history—even though many people may not readily recall his name.

He played in the 1940s, a decade featuring more high-profile quarterbacks like Sammy Baugh in Washington and Sid Luckman in Chicago. But for a period in the late 1940s, Thompson was as good, if not better, than them all. And with Thompson running coach Earle "Greasy" Neale's T formation, the Eagles enjoyed the franchise's first sustained success.

It all began in 1941 with the infamous franchise swap between Bert Bell and Art Rooney, who owned the Eagles, and Alexis Thompson, who owned the Steelers at the time. They switched team ownership, and Neale moved over as Philly's coach and brought a strong-armed, cocky quarterback, Thompson, with him.

Hard to Say Goodbye

Tommy Thompson was nothing if not a creature of habit.

From his days when he first started playing football on the Kansas prairie to his days at the University of Tulsa to his NFL days in Pittsburgh and then Philadelphia, he always used the same pair of shoulder pads.

After the 1948 season Eagles equipment manager Fred Schubach sent all the team's equipment away to be repaired at a leather factory. He soon got a note back from the factory on Thompson's shoulder pads: "Rejected. This article is too far gone to justify the expense of reconditioning it."

Bemused, Schubach put the ancient pads and the note back in Thompson's locker. When he saw it, the quarterback just laughed. "These pads are the best in the world," he said. "They get better every year."

The two men enjoyed something of a love/hate relationship throughout their time together, but Neale knew Thompson could run his misdirection better than just about anyone else.

But after two seasons, World War II called, and Thompson served two years, earning a Purple Heart as part of the second wave of U.S. soldiers who landed at Normandy on D-Day. He was back in time for part of the 1945 season before rounding back into form in 1946, when he led the league by completing nearly 56 percent of his passes.

By 1947 Thompson finally had the offensive weapons around him, including wide receiver Pete Pihos, that finally made the Eagles a force to be reckoned with. They reached the NFL Championship Game that season, and Thompson completed what was then a record 27 of 44 passes in a tough 28–21 loss to the Chicago Cardinals.

The next season, the Eagles were back, thanks to Thompson, who threw for 1,965 yards and an incredible 25 touchdown passes, a team record that stood until 1961. That was the year, with the likes of Steve Van Buren and Pihos, that the Eagles finally won it all, beating the Cardinals 7–0 in a howling Philadelphia blizzard.

Thompson threw for another 1,700 yards and 16 touchdowns the following season as the Eagles defended their NFL title, this time beating the Rams.

In that three-year period from 1947 to 1949 Thompson threw 661 passes and only had 37 intercepted—an impressive statistic for that era. Thompson, in fact, detested interceptions, calling them the single most important play a defense can make.

That was the Eagles' heyday. In 1950 they slipped to 6–6 and Neale was fired after the season. Thompson also decided he'd had enough and retired. He went on to coach at the University of Arkansas and in the Canadian Football League.

He died in 1989 of brain cancer, still considered one the greatest quarterbacks in team history.

90 Marty Mornhinweg

When the 2010 season ended, Marty Mornhinweg's name rose to the top of the list of potential head-coaching candidates. And there were a number of openings that year, openings that Mornhinweg, who had just finished his eighth season as an assistant coach with the Eagles and his fifth as offensive coordinator, seemed perfect for.

There were the Denver Broncos and the Carolina Panthers and the Oakland Raiders and what looked like the best bet of all, the Cleveland Browns—where his mentor and friend, Mike Holmgren, was the team president.

But all those teams hired somebody else, and Mornhinweg was left to wait for another opportunity. It was nothing new for the fiery coach who played quarterback in high school and college and learned his coaching craft at six different colleges before getting his breakthrough on the NFL level. He learned offense from some of the best minds in the game and took what he learned, sprinkled in some of his own philosophy, and earned the respect of just about every player he tutored. "Whatever I've accomplished, it's because of Marty," Eagles quarterback Michael Vick said at the end of the 2010 season. "I hope he gets another chance to be a head coach. He deserves it."

Another chance. There's the rub. In 2001 Mornhinweg, in a move that stunned just about everyone, was named head coach of the Detroit Lions. And though he'd coached 16 seasons, including the previous four as offensive coordinator of the San Francisco 49ers, he'd never been a head coach anywhere.

For some neophyte head coaches, that's not an issue. Unfortunately for Mornhinweg, it was. In two disastrous, forgettable seasons, the Lions lost 27 of 32 games, and Mornhinweg made enough mistakes to last a lifetime.

Perhaps his most famous blunder came in a 2002 game against the Chicago Bears. The game was tied and went into overtime, where the Lions won the crucial coin toss. But instead of taking the ball, Mornhinweg decided on the windy Chicago afternoon to kick to the Bears in hopes of forcing them to make a mistake. They didn't. The Bears kept the ball, kicked a field goal, won the game, and enraged Lions fans. After two seasons, he was fired.

But he didn't stay unemployed for long. His good friend, Eagles head coach Andy Reid, scooped him up immediately and made a senior assistant. In 2004 he was named assistant head coach, and two years later, he assumed the title of offensive coordinator/ assistant head coach.

Mornhinweg evolved as Reid's right-hand man, even calling plays in certain games. He helped the Eagles offense gain some diversity and splash, especially in 2010 when Vick assumed

Donovan McNabb (left) clowns around with Eagles offensive coordinator Marty Mornhinweg during the morning session of football training camp at Lehigh University in Bethlehem, Pennsylvania, on July 27, 2009.

control of the offense. Indeed, from 2008 to 2010, the Eagles set franchise records for points scored. For his part, Mornhinweg said he is content to wait for another opportunity to be a head coach.

His former boss, Reid, is convinced his friend will get that chance. "I think he deserves that opportunity," he said. "There are some great second-time head coaches out there, with Bill Belichick and Tom Coughlin being two of the great ones."

Mornhinweg has yet to get that second opportunity, but he has remained solidly entrenched in the NFL. He left the Eagles after the 2012 season and became offensive coordinator for the New York Jets for two years. In 2015, he joined the Baltimore Ravens as quarterbacks coach and was eventually elevated to offensive coordinator.

91 Hoagiegate

In Philadelphia, you simply don't mess with the hoagie. It is to this town what cheese is to Wisconsin, what wine is to San Francisco, and what coffee is to Seattle...but even more important.

First, a little history lesson for the uninitiated. In other parts of the country, this particular sandwich may be know as a *hero*, while in other parts it's a *submarine*, and yet in another it could be a *grinder*. But to Philly natives, the hoagie is a singular sandwich, created and perfected in their town. We've all had one—no matter what it was called. It's various types of meat, cheese, and lettuce on Italian bread.

The most common explanation for the unusual name "hoagie" seems to center on the Philadelphia shipyards around World War I, when Italian immigrants were hired to work on emergency shipping for the war effort. The shipyard was known as Hog Island, and when the Italian immigrants brought these sandwiches to work, they were nicknamed "Hog Island sandwiches"—or hoagies. It's probably as good as any explanation, but the point is that Philadelphians embraced these sandwiches like nothing else.

By the 1950s they were served everywhere, and while the spellings might have differed from neighborhood to neighborhood, the passion did not.

Former Philadelphia mayor and later governor of Pennsylvania Ed Rendell even went so far as to the declare the hoagie the "Official Sandwich of Philadelphia." So this was clearly a serious subject.

Not surprisingly, Eagles fans and food go hand in hand, and in a tradition that stretched back to the dawn of the team in 1933, fans were always allowed to bring food into the stadium with them. The favored item? Hoagies, of course!

No one thought too much about it until 2003, when the Eagles prepared to move into their new playground, Lincoln Financial Field. In July, just weeks before the Eagles' first game in the new ballpark, the team announced that fans would no longer be able to bring their own food into the stadium. And, just like that, a tradition was abandoned. To the surprise of no one except perhaps the Eagles front office, the city went crazy. Dubbed "Hoagiegate," everyone took a side in this burgeoning food fight.

The Eagles tried to explain that this was a chance for fans to enjoy a truly memorable experience at the stadium. There would be food of all kinds, in a great atmosphere and for fans to enjoy whenever they wanted. They also cited security issues as a reason for not allowing unauthorized food into the park.

Philly fans made the excellent argument that they brought their own food for the simple reason they didn't want to spend a fortune on stadium concessions. As for security, few fans had ever seen a loaded hoagie.

In the ensuing weeks, pictures of team owner Jeff Lurie could be found with hoagies sticking out of each of his ears with the simply slogan, "Stuff it." Season-ticket holders cancelled their plans, and other threatened to boycott games.

Finally, in early August, the Eagles relented...sort of. They would allow fans to bring food into the stadium as they always had, but they would have to enter through specific gates so their goods could be inspected.

The news was so important that Rendell, by this point the governor, made the announcement from his office in Harrisburg.

The great sandwich war was over before it had begun. And, fortunately, with only a few casualties.

92 Hot and Pickled

You've heard of the Ice Bowl, when the Green Bay Packers took their place in legend and lore and mysticism by beating the Dallas Cowboys in the 1967 NFL Championship Game at Lambeau Field, where the temperature sunk to a knee-cracking 15 below zero. You remember San Diego Chargers quarterback Dan Fouts crumbling on the Riverfront Stadium field in the AFC Championship Game against the Cincinnati Bengals.

In pro football, it's the games played in the numbing cold that seem to find their way into history. It's man against the elements—and when man wins, or at least plays it even, that's a story that transcends the decades.

But what about games played in the stifling heat? Those games when simply moving causes a player to lose another pint of fluid? For some reason, they're not quite so dramatic, are they?

The Philadelphia Eagles found themselves in the middle of one of those. And while most folks outside Philly don't remember, it remains a pleasant memory for those who call themselves true Eagles fans.

It was September 3, 2000, and the Eagles played their season opener in Dallas against the hated Cowboys. Never a bargain weatherwise between May and October anyway, the Texas heat settled in with a vengeance on this afternoon. The game-time temperature was a set-your-hair-on-fire 109 degrees. That was bad enough. But on the artificial turf of Texas Stadium, the heat rose to an ungodly 150 degrees. But this was the NFL, and you played.

And while it seemed the Cowboys, who lived and practiced in the sauna, would benefit from the hot weather, it was the Eagles—and an ingenious idea from their head trainer—that turned the tables.

It really began in training camp when trainer Steve Burkholder recommended players drink two-ounce shots of pickle juice to reduce dehydration. Not only that, the "juice" made players even more thirsty, so they drank more water and stayed hydrated.

Most of the Eagles took to the idea, though a few, like quarterback Donovan McNabb, declined. Nonetheless, as the Eagles prepared for the season opener in the furnace of east Texas, they were more prepared than their rivals. They were hydrated, relaxed, and confident, and it showed.

Burkholder deserved even more credit because he suggested to coach Andy Reid that the team cut short is pregame warmup to stay fresh. Reid agreed, and while the Cowboys practiced in the heat, the Eagles stayed cool in their locker room. The results were dramatic. Running back Duce Staley ran for a career-best 201 yards, and the Eagles crushed Dallas 41–14.

That the Eagles thrived in the heat was only one surprise. That win all but signaled the end of the Cowboys' reign in the NFC and demonstrated that the Eagles, under second-year coach Reid, were ready to assume control of the NFC East.

And it all started with a little pickle juice.

93 Bill Hewitt

He may have been the last of the NFL's truly tough guys. But Bill Hewitt was no throwback, he was an original, created and forged in the raucous, outlaw early days of the NFL.

Even today, the Hall of Famer is remembered for his stubborn refusal to wear a helmet. Of course, even in his day, helmets were leather and provided almost no protection from the pounding players took every week. But at least they were something.

Hewitt hailed from tough Bay City, Michigan, and played his college ball at the University of Michigan, where he didn't make much of an impact.

But when he got to the NFL and played for the Chicago Bears, it was a different story. In his first seven seasons, playing both offense and defense, he was named All-NFL four times. He averaged more than 50 minutes per game, playing quarterback on offense and lineman on defense. Indeed, his reaction to the ball was so quick on defense that he was nicknamed "the Offside Kid" because he moved so fast.

In 1937 he joined the Eagles, then only in their fifth year of existence. Coach and owner Bert Bell was so happy to have him, he doubled Hewitt's salary to $200 per game and arranged a $24-a-week off-season job for him as a service-station mechanic.

The Eagles still weren't any good on the field, but Hewitt, now the only player in the league who didn't wear a helmet, was the star.

The Eagles won just two of 11 games that season, but Hewitt was the key in both victories—upset wins over the powerful Washington Redskins and Brooklyn Dodgers. Hewitt scored one touchdown and set up a second in a 14–0 win over Washington and scored once in a 14–10 conquest of the Dodgers.

He was named All-NFL again with the Eagles in 1937 and 1938, becoming the first player ever to earn that honor with two different teams.

But by 1939 the league powers that be finally laid down the law. That season, every player was required to wear a helmet, and Hewitt's days as the last tough guy were over. He retired after that season but returned in 1943 to join the Steagles for their one interesting season.

He again retired after that season but, tragically, was killed in a car wreck in 1947. He was inducted into the Pro Football Hall of Fame in 1971.

94 Tony Franklin

In 1979, even as today, it was a risk of epic proportions to take a kicker early in the draft. Kickers, by their very nature, were flighty and unpredictable and, all too frequently, marched to their own drummer. So if a team risked a valuable early pick on a kicker who didn't succeed, it could set a franchise back at least a year—if not longer. But in 1979 the Eagles really had no choice. They had gone through four kickers in the previous two seasons, and the lack of a credible field-goal threat was a constant source of aggravation to coach Dick Vermeil.

Indeed, Vermeil was convinced all the pieces were in place for his team to be a legitimate Super Bowl contender; all he needed was a kicker he could count on.

So in that year's draft, the Eagles front office closed their eyes, collectively held their breath, and selected Tony Franklin—a rocket-legged barefoot kicker from Texas A&M—with their third-round pick.

It immediately paid dividends. In that first season, Franklin hit 23 of 31 field goals and scored 105 points, more than the previous two Eagles kickers had scored combined. He brought accuracy, security, and an arrogance rarely seen in someone who kicks balls for a living.

That point was driven home that first season when the Eagles traveled to Dallas in November to face the powerful Cowboys, a team they had lost to nine straight times.

Vermeil knew the Eagles would go nowhere until they found a way to beat the Cowboys, and it was their little kicker who gave the Eagles the confidence to do it.

During pregame warm-ups, Franklin boomed his kickoffs right into the area where the Cowboys were warming up. Kick after kick landed in their area, and several Cowboys warned the rookie to cut it out. He didn't. It was a statement from someone who probably didn't know any better that he was not going to be intimidated—even by the Cowboys.

More important, during the game, with just seconds left before halftime, the Eagles faced fourth down and what amounted to a 59-yard field goal. Cowboys coach Tom Landry figured Franklin didn't have the leg for a kick that far and declined a five-yard penalty on the Eagles. Franklin went up to Vermeil and said, "Coach, I can hit that." Vermeil responded simply, "Go ahead."

Franklin's kick cleared the crossbar with five yards to spare and gave the Eagles an emotional charge that carried them for the rest of the game. Philly snapped their five-season losing streak to the Cowboys and won 31–21.

Franklin helped beat the Cowboys one more time the following season, in the NFC Championship Game that sent the Eagles to the Super Bowl.

Franklin kicked four more seasons for the Eagles, scoring 412 points, before he was traded to the New England Patriots in 1984. He played there for four seasons and then played for the Miami Dolphins in 1988.

He now lives in San Antonio, Texas, and works in the financial field. In his free time he does color commentary for local Texas high school football.

95 Tom Woodeshick

If there was ever a player born and bred to play for the Philadelphia Eagles, it was Tom "Woody" Woodeshick, a fullback with only marginal skills who made the most of every ounce of talent he could squeeze from his body.

Born in Wilkes-Barre, Pennsylvania, north of Philadelphia, he played college ball not far away at West Virginia University. Woody never shied away from the fact that he was the perfect player for the Eagles. "Who wants to play in San Francisco or New York, someplace like that?" he said at one time. "This is where I belong. [Eagles fans] cheered me as a rookie, and I only carried the ball five times. They love me, and I love them."

Love? Eagles fans? It's a concept few players can wrap their heads around, but Woodeshick had that everyman quality that Philly fans truly loved. An eighth-round draft choice of the Eagles in 1963 (he was also a fourth-round selection of the AFL's Buffalo Bills, but he chose the more established NFL), he was never really supposed to provide much more than a few carries on offense and some tackles on special teams.

Teammate Bob Brown, an offensive tackle who opened a number of holes for Woodeshick, called him the toughest fullback of the era. "And this was the era of [Cleveland star] Jim Brown," Brown said. "Some guys talk tough and act tough. Other guys play tough and are tough. That was Woody."

But Woodeshick had more than guts and determination. As it turned out, he was a pretty fair running back as well. And in 1968 he had a chance to prove it. That season the Eagles were awful again, but Woodeshick was the lone bright spot running the ball and had a chance to gain 1,000 yards for the season as the season finale against the Vikings loomed.

Remember, it was a 14-game schedule then, and a 1,000-yard season was a much bigger deal than it is today with the 16-game schedule. And Woody had a chance to crack that barrier even after missing most of a game earlier in the season when he was thrown out for fighting with the Cowboys' Mike Gaechter.

In the third quarter of the finale, Woodeshick was just 53 yards shy of the magic mark when disaster struck. At the end of a run, Woodeshick was hit so hard by Minnesota linebacker Lonnie Warwick that his face mask cracked. A jagged piece flew up and cut Woodeshick on the left eyelid, sending out a torrent of blood and forcing him from the game.

Woodeshick was so obsessed with the 1,000-yard barrier that he begged the doctor to let him return, even as the doctor was trying to stitch the wound. The doctor as adamant and would not let him return. "Do you want to lose that eye?" the doctor asked.

"I didn't care," Woodeshick said later. "I worked so hard to get to that point. I knew there was a good chance I'd never get that close again."

He was right. Woody finished that season with 947 yards, still the most by an Eagles back since Steve Van Buren's 1,146 yards in 1949. And while he was named to the Pro Bowl for the first and only time of his career, the lost opportunity stayed with him for years.

He had another good season in 1969, rushing for 831 yards, but a knee injury in 1970 ended the magic-carpet ride. He played one more season for the St. Louis Cardinals and retired, having rushed for 3,577 yards and 21 touchdowns. Not bad for a guy who wasn't supposed to even make the team. But his love of the game and determination to be the best he could possibly be was never lost on teammates, opponents, or real fans of the NFL.

Once he told Gordon Forbes of *USA Today*, "Let's face it, once you put on that uniform and go on the field, it's no place for anyone but madmen."

96 The Praying Tailback

It's a fairly common sight in today's NFL. Players who reach the end zone, make a big play, kick a field goal, or otherwise do something extraordinary on the field can be seen looking to the heavens or kneeling in prayer in an act of appreciation.

But it had to start somewhere. One player had to take that first step and do what other players had probably thought to do but never seriously considered. Herb Lusk did, and in an October 9, 1977, game against the New York Giants, the Eagles halfback put his unflinching religious beliefs into practice.

A relatively unremarkable college back from Long Beach State, Lusk was a 10th-round draft pick of the Eagles in 1976 who told the team at the time that if he made the roster, he would only play

Unbeknownst to him at the time, Herb Lusk starts a widespread football trend here in 1977.

three seasons. After that, he would follow in his father's footsteps and become a minister.

And he did. After three solid, if unspectacular, seasons in Philadelphia, he did indeed walk away and start his ministry work, which he continues to this day.

But he will always be remembered for what he did in that game in 1977 when he took a pitch from quarterback Ron Jaworski, turned the left corner, and ran untouched for a 70-yard touchdown at the Meadowlands. Once in the end zone, he dropped to his left knee, bowed his head briefly, got up, and went to the sideline. "It was just my way of saying thanks," said Lusk, who had badly injured his knee in college and was told he may never play again.

But he said he prayed and God healed his knee. "It was God's will that I keep playing football," he said, and his prayer after the touchdown was his acknowledgement.

It was the start of a tradition followed by many players since then, though interestingly, it was not remarked on by any of the media in attendance.

All of Lusk's teammates knew how religious he was and were not surprised by his demonstration. "We thought, *That's Herb,*" Jaworski said at the time. But from then on, Lusk was known as "the Praying Tailback," a moniker he did not mind at all.

"That day is pretty much a blur to me." Lusk told the *Washington Post* 30 years later. "But I'm very proud of when I look and see guys praying in the end zone and praying after [a game]. I see these guys as my sons. I gave birth to them. I see that as my purpose for playing in the NFL."

Lusk scored three NFL touchdowns in his brief career and knelt after all three. He left football and had been since 1982 senior pastor of the Greater Exodus Baptist Church in North Philadelphia.

Every day, people still ask him about his days as "the Praying Tailback," and he always smiles.

"I was the first," he said.

97 Edwin "Alabama" Pitts

Brief and controversial, but oh-so-entertaining, that was the life and Eagles career of one Edwin "Alabama" Pitts, the first and last Eagles player who joined the team after a stint in the big house.

In truth, Pitts was nothing more than a novelty act for the Eagles, a franchise that was just two years old and still trying to generate word of mouth and ticket sales. Team owner Bert Bell, with grudging support from coach Lud Wray, thought signing Pitts would be exactly what the team needed.

But first things first. Pitts was born in Alabama and, so he could be distinguished from his father who was also named Edwin, his mother nicknamed him "Alabama." He joined the Navy at age 15, but after he was discharged three years later, he bounced around, unable to land steady work.

Desperate for money, the 19-year-old kid agreed to take part in a holdup of a New York City grocery store that netted $78.25, not an insignificant amount in 1929. But Pitts and his three accomplices were caught and sentenced to eight to 15 years in Sing Sing, the notorious prison in New York state.

While at Sing Sing, Pitts joined the prison football and baseball teams and was far and away the best athlete. After five years, Pitts was eligible for parole, and former Chicago Cubs star Johnny Evers, who was then managing a minor league team in Albany, New York, took up his cause. Evers offered Pitts $200 a month to play for him, a deal challenged by the league because of its unwillingness to let a convicted felon into its sport.

The case made it all the way to baseball commissioner Kenesaw Mountain Landis, who ruled in Pitts' favor. His performance on the field was something less than spectacular, but from afar, Bert

Bell saw the excitement Pitts' case was generating and decided to get into the action. In September 1935 Bell signed Pitts to a $1,500 contract to play running back in four exhibition games and four regular-season games. It was an unheard-of offer for a player who (A) had never played organized football before and (B) was a paroled felon.

But the move had the desired effect for the Eagles. Published reports at the time said 20,000 fans showed up to watch the Eagles' home opener against Pittsburgh—four times the normal attendance. Throughout the entire game, fans clamored for Pitts to get into the action, but Wray, convinced Pitts did not have the necessary skills, wouldn't put him in.

He did play briefly in the next two games, and in the final game of his contract—against the Chicago Bears—he caught two passes for 21 yards. Offered a new contract for considerably less money, Pitts refused and went back to baseball, where he banged around in the minor leagues and then in semipro ball.

In 1941, after an altercation at a bar in North Carolina, Pitts was stabbed and died. He was just 33.

For years, Pitts was listed in the *Eagles Media Guide*'s all-time roster as having attended Sing Sing. In 2000 it was changed to "no college."

98 Kevin Turner

There was a time—and it's probably forgotten by most Eagles fans—when Kevin Turner was the second-best fullback in the NFL. Tough and relentless, the University of Alabama product would stick his head in anywhere and do whatever was necessary to get the job done. And in the end, that ability is what will likely kill him.

"I never thought about my head, the way I was abusing my head, the pounding my head was taking, and the long-term consequences," Turner told ESPN.com recently.

He knows now. In August 2010, at age 41, Turner was diagnosed with amyotrophic lateral sclerosis, more commonly known as Lou Gehrig's Disease. It's an incurable neuromuscular disorder that will rob Turner of his motor functions and will, eventually, kill him. One doctor told him he had 10 years to live; a second told him he had five, and a third said two. "I'm going to stop going to the doctors," he cracked.

But Turner is convinced ALS was caused by years of collisions. Indeed, in 2010, he was the 16th former NFL player diagnosed with the relatively rare disease. One former Chicago Bears safety, Dave Duerson, committed suicide, actually shooting himself in the chest so doctors could study his brain for valuable research. "When I retired, doctors told me I had the spinal column of a 65-year-old man," he said.

Today, Turner said if he knew then what he knows now, he never would have played football. But he didn't. In fact, for eight seasons, including five with the Eagles, he was the epitome of what a fullback was supposed to be.

He was a third-round draft pick of the New England Patriots in 1992 and, in 1994, he enjoyed a career year, catching 52 passes for 471 yards and scoring three touchdowns. A tough runner with great hands for a fullback, Turner made himself into the kind of versatile player teams covet. "They don't make fullbacks like him anymore," Patriots coach Bill Parcells said at the time.

But in 1995 Turner signed with the Eagles—a three-year deal worth $4.125 million, which made him the second-highest-paid fullback in the league behind Dallas' Daryl Johnston.

Turner never found the same success in his five years in Philly that he did in New England, but he still had a solid career. His best season with the Eagles was 1997, when he caught 48 passes for 443 yards and rushed for another 96 yards.

But it was also that season, in a September game against the Packers at Veterans Stadium, when Turner took a vicious hit to the head. On the sideline, Turner asked backup quarterback Bobby Hoying if they were playing the game in Green Bay or in Philadelphia. "I looked around the stadium and couldn't tell," he said.

Injuries finally caught up with him, and Turner retired after the 1999 season having caught 138 passes for the Eagles. It was a few years late that evidence of neuromuscular problems started to develop. He was already losing the use of his arms and, after his diagnosis in 2010, he was told by doctors that his speech would probably go next.

Now he has gone public about his ALS and is campaigning for stricter control of head injuries and for the NFL to take the issue of concussions more seriously. He knows it's too late for him, but he hopes his plight will educate others.

"Nobody can see the future," he said. "For me, it just falls into a long line of bad decisions."

On March 24, 2016, Turner died from what everyone assumed was complications from ALS. But upon studying his brain (which he had agreed to donate upon his death), it was learned he actually died from chronic traumatic encephalopathy (CTE), the disease associated with constant head trauma. Turner's donation is another step in medical science journey to understand the impact of collisions of athletes' brains.

99 Rich Kotite

The numbers say one thing; the perception says something else.

For many Eagles fans, the four-year tenure of Rich Kotite as head coach was an unmitigated disaster: bad football, bad attitudes, bad performances, bad...everything.

But was that really the case? In his four seasons, Kotite, the tough-talking Brooklyn native, led the Eagles to a 37–29 record, including a playoff victory. Not bad for most coaches, especially after dealing with a rash of injuries to key players and losing top defensive player Reggie White to free agency.

But what sticks with most Eagles fans is how Kotite lost control of his team in 1994 and watched a 7–2 season collapse with seven straight losses.

Was Kotite a good coach caught in bad circumstances, or was he a bad coach who couldn't motivate players? Probably, he was a little bit of both. But this much is clear: Kotite's reputation in Philly hasn't really improved over the years.

He was brought to Philadelphia by then-owner Norman Braman in 1991 to do two things: win playoff games and clean up the team's bad-boy image, which had been nurtured by the man he replaced, Buddy Ryan.

Kotite indeed instilled more discipline and accountability. Where Ryan ran his ship loosely, Kotite required much more, going so far as to demand that his players line up in numerical order on the sideline during the national anthem. He also closed practice to fans and media, another major departure from Ryan.

And while he projected a tough-guy image (he once sparred with Muhammad Ali), he also knew his football. He had played for the Pittsburgh Steelers and New York Giants and was an assistant coach in New Orleans and with the New York Jets before joining Ryan as the Eagles' offensive coordinator in 1990.

But this was Kotite's first head-coaching gig, and he never figured out what it took to combine the discipline he demanded with the respect he needed.

Yet Kotite's first two seasons were just fine—the Eagles were 10–6 in 1991 despite losing starting quarterback Randall Cunningham to a knee injury in the first game. In 1992 Philly posted an 11–5 mark and beat New Orleans in the first round of the playoffs—the Eagles' first playoff win since the 1980 season.

But it started going south in 1993. Reggie White left via free agency, Cunningham got hurt again and, after a 4–0 start, the Eagles stumbled to an 8–8 season.

Then in 1994, Jeffrey Lurie bought the Eagles from Braman and wasn't sure Kotite was the man he wanted in charge of his new investment. The Eagles roared out to a 7–2 start, but after beating the Arizona Cardinals on November 6, the Eagles did not win again, losing their last seven. It was the first time in NFL history a team had started 7–2 and finished under .500.

That was clearly the last straw for Lurie. But the pressure had been building for a long time. Many players thought Kotite had diluted the Eagles. He may have cleaned up the bad-boy image, but he had made the team colorless and boring.

He was also viewed as a poor game manager and, worse, a bad evaluator of talent. In his four seasons, Kotite drafted 41 players, and only 20 were still on the roster at the end of the 1994 season.

Two days after the 1994 season ended, Lurie fired Kotite and replaced him with Ray Rhodes. Kotite's next stop was as head coach of the New York Jets, where it got even worse. In two seasons, his teams won just four games. He was fired after the 1996 season.

He never coached again and now works in media as a regular contributor to NFL Films and the NFL Network.

100 Shibe Park

The place looked old even when it was new. Built in 1909 for the old Philadelphia Athletics baseball team and named for A's owner Benjamin Shibe, the park cost $377,000 and covered a city block in North Philly at 21st Street and Lehigh Avenue.

It was considered a state-of-the-art facility at the time and was the first ballpark built of concrete and steel. Before that, most professional stadiums were made of wood. Still, Shibe Park was an imposing edifice, gray and black and fearsome-looking. It was also witness to some terrific athletic events.

Shibe Park was the first long-term home to the Philadelphia Eagles. For their first three years, from 1933 to 1935 the Eagles had played at the cramped, tiny, crumbling Baker Bowl. From 1936 to 1939 they played in the more spacious, more modern Municipal Stadium. But when the city wanted to raise the rent on the Eagles to play there, team owner Bert Bell took his team up the road to Shibe Park, a stadium more suited for baseball.

The A's president, Connie Mack, offered a backhanded welcome to the new tenants and their fledgling sport. Questioned about whether the stadium's lights were good enough for the NFL, Mack said, "If our lights are good enough to play baseball at its best, they certainly are going to be more than satisfactory for football."

Ouch.

Configured to seat 33,000 for baseball and 39,000 for football, the park rarely saw sellouts for the Eagles, though it was the site of one of the Eagles' two NFL Championship Game wins and three division titles.

And while it had pleasant memories in that regard, the fact remained, Shibe Park was never meant for football. The biggest problem? Without question, it was the field itself. Former Eagles lineman Marion Campbell once cracked, "The field was so bad, you could've played hockey and basketball on it and not hurt it. Late in the season, you couldn't put a hole in that field with a jack-hammer. Our locker room? I don't think we had one."

It was a fairly common complaint about most NFL stadiums of the day—many of which have to be carved out of existing baseball stadiums that had far different sightlines.

The Eagles beat the Chicago Cardinals 7–0 in the 1948 NFL Championship Game on December 19, 1948, at Shibe Park in Philly.

The field itself was so bad that frequently coach Greasy Neal ewould take his team across the street to practice instead of subjecting his players to the Shibe Park turf.

Shibe Park was renamed Connie Mack Stadium in 1953, but the A's left for Kansas City in 1954. The Eagles stayed, but that didn't alleviate the issues that still plagued the stadium.

In the 1950s the biggest concern was parking—or the lack thereof. Downtown parking was tough enough to find and, where it was located, getting out was even worse with the congestion of thousands of cars trying to go to the same place.

"We're in the auto age," team president Frank McNamee said in 1956. "People want the maximum of comfort, and if we want them to come out, we have to give it to them."

Finally in 1958 the Eagles announced they were leaving the old ballpark for the larger, more modern Franklin Field.

Shibe Park may have been uncomfortable and small and not suited to watching football, but in the 18 seasons they played there, the Eagles were 57–35–6.

The stadium was damaged by a fire in 1971 and was demolished in 1976. And all that remains are the memories.

Sources

Didinger, Ray, and Robert Lyons. The Eagles Encyclopedia. Philadelphia: Temple University Press, 2005.

Gordon, Bob. *Game of My Life: Philadelphia Eagles: Memorable Stories of Eagles Football.* Champaign, IL: Sports Publishing LLC, 2007.